POSSESS YOUR SUCCESS

MASTERING THE LIMITLESS SUCCESS METHOD

ANDREW G. MCDONALD

Possess Your Success:
Mastering the Limitless Success Method

©Andrew McDonald 2016

Although the author and publisher have made every effort to ensure that the information in this book was correct at press time, the author and publisher do not assume and hereby disclaim any liability to any party for any loss, damage, or disruption caused by errors or omissions, whether such errors or omissions result from negligence, accident, or any other cause.

For author and speaker bookings visit possessyoursuccess.com

CONTENTS

Introduction..1
The First Step..7
Failing to Succeed..25
Fear's Bad Rap..35
Everything Begins with a Thought............................45
Thoughts are Seeds...64
Behold the Power of Words.......................................73
The 5 Essential Forces of Success.............................92
Take the Leap...122
Conclusion: How to Enjoy Your Success..................139

To God, my source.
To my wife, my unshakable rock.
To my family, friends, and fans, my support in trying times.
To Grace, a complete stranger who helped make this possible.

This is for you.

Introduction

When I first began the journey of writing a book, I knew I had amazing revelations to share and a powerful overall message to deliver. I have been studying the behaviors of successful people over the past several years. Where do they get their motivation to succeed when others sputter into inaction? How do they have the ability to achieve, time and time again, while others have more credentials or skills? What do they study and how do they divide their time to maximize their potential? In short, what are they doing to consistently succeed that the rest of us are not?

Then I asked myself the same questions. As a highly motivated individual, I have often wondered where I got my go-getter attitude. While I always believed myself to be a smart individual, intelligence by no means guarantees success or provides motivation to prosper. In fact, I know plenty who are smarter than me, yet never quite realized their full potential. I also knew it wasn't religion-specific, either. Religious people can struggle or thrive just as much as the non-religious do, although I know firsthand that religious principles, when used effectively, do work.

Thus, what I did was analyze both the spiritual and secular aspects of success and motivation to find the commonalities shared between them. I realized that many of the success principles between the two groups are not mutually exclusive; that is, they are actually one and the same. Faith is faith, whether you believe in one God, many gods, or no gods at all. If you give, other people are likely to give back greater than you initially gave. Whether you believe it is by divine favor or random luck, some are afforded opportunities that others are not. However, everyone at some point is presented opportunities to succeed, and it is what people do with these opportunities that determines just how far they can go. The steps in what I call the "Limitless Success Method" will help you take advantage of such opportunities.

I'd like to take this moment to level with you: the principles outlined in the Limitless Success Method are not new. However, they are still relevant, timeless ideologies that have been consistently and successfully used to build empires of riches, prosperity, and fulfillment. In fact, they have been utilized by notable leaders, celebrities, and entrepreneurs from Walt Disney to Andrew Carnegie, all the way to Oprah Winfrey. These principles can work for the poor to attain wealth, as well as for the wealthy to protect and grow their wealth. They are very versatile and can be used to achieve success in a multitude of areas, including health, wealth, career advancement, personal development, and interpersonal relationships. In reality, the only limits placed on these principles are the ones used by the reader of this book. They have been written and spoken about exhaustively in many literary works, but never quite packaged together and broken down like in this book. I advise using these principles in *every* facet of your life. Hold nothing back.

To effectively understand and utilize the Limitless Success Method, I begin with the prep work and factors to consider when taking the first step towards your success. This prep work is not optional; it is vital to take each point to heart and incorporate it into your overall success strategy. The second, third, and fourth chapters may not guarantee success (nothing ever will), but it will make success much more achievable and likely. Otherwise, your success journey will be held up by obstacles at nearly every turn.

POSSESS YOUR SUCCESS: MASTERING THE LIMITLESS SUCESS METHOD

From there, I then explain in detail the three steps to the Limitless Success Method. These three steps are simple to remember but will require a lot of effort and diligence on your part to implement. They are as follows: "Think It. Speak It. Do It." The first step, "Think It," will prepare your mind for success. To do this, I will show you how to renew your mind, think thoughts of success, and defend your mind from negative thoughts, self-doubt, and your emotions all in an effort to recognize the opportunities around you. Moreover, I discuss at length the difference between the Limited, those who place limits on themselves and their success, and the Limitless, those who transcend any previous limitations set upon them. Once you have the "Think It" step down, opportunities will seem to appear out of thin air, and while they have always been there, you will now have the mental fortitude to recognize and take advantage of them.

The second step of the Limitless Success Method, "Speak It," will prepare your words for Limitless success. Thinking positive thoughts is nice, but there is considerable power in the words you speak or that are spoken to you. Speaking words, whether positive or negative, out loud and in a consistent manner will actually override your thoughts and cause you to think in line with them. I also explain that if you speak your intentions into the universe actively and consistently over time, the universe will have no choice but to bring you what you desire. From there, it is up to you to take advantage of it.

This is where the final section of the book, "Do It," is most useful. Many individuals believe that with the right attitude and positive words alone, good things will happen. Unfortunately, in my experience this has led to nothing but disempowerment of the individual because there has been no action taken on their part to succeed. You have been empowered with the innate ability to succeed, but you have to take some corresponding action to see consistent success in your life. Without the works, your faith is powerless.

However, taking action is easier said than done. That is why, in this section, I leave you with the 5 Essential Forces of Success that everyone Limitlessly successful will embody. Applying these principles in your implementation plan will bolster your success in ways you never thought possible. Finally, if you believe you are ready to take that leap and have instilled the Limitless Success Method in yourself, I provide you with additional factors to reflect on to determine your readiness and willingness to step off that ledge, as well as how to do it in a safe and effective manner.

To conclude the book, I explain why success needs to be enjoyed. I know it may seem silly, but many successful people (myself included) have trouble taking time to appreciate the work we have put in, as well as the results we have achieved, because we are too focused on the next goal. This will eventually lead to burnout and abandonment of your goals and dreams altogether. Instead, I detail what you need to do to actually appreciate the success you achieve, because life is too short not to enjoy yourself along the way.

Now, some skeptics might feel that this could be just another "woo woo" feel-good book filled with unsubstantiated claims and opinions. This simply isn't true. While many other books offer inspiring, energetic motivation without the tools necessary to achieve success or hard data to support their positions, I refuse to deliver such a disempowering message. In fact, while I do provide uplifting ideas and points, I use scholarly research articles to support them and the practical methods to implement them. The most frustrating experience when beginning a quest is to be motivated to take action and yet not know how to do so. Furthermore, this is not:

- *A "get rich quick" book.* Although you can apply the Limitless Success Method to achieve a high degree of wealth, by no means will it be a quick journey, and the book is not solely focused on finances.

- *A religious self-help book.* This book is written fully in line with my Christian values, yet it is certainly agnostic. This is the advantage of the Limitless Success Method: no matter what or whom you believe in, every step will apply to you.

- *A book that defines success for you.* It is not my intention to define what success is in your life. As I explain in Chapter 2, success is unique to every individual and you must seek to possess *your* success, not anyone else's.

- *A book on material success as a means to happiness.* Along with the point above, if you define success in terms of material possessions, it is possible to achieve it and still not be happy. This book only defines the steps necessary to make success a consistent occurrence in your life.

- *A book that teaches you to eliminate or avoid failure.* Failure is a necessary part of the Limitless Success Method. Therefore I teach how to "fail to succeed," using your failures to learn and grow. Readers will come to realize that failure should be embraced, not avoided.

ANDREW G. MCDONALD

    This is it. This is Limitless success, boiled down to three steps and an abundance of tools to get you to the next level. If you sincerely take this book to heart and approach it with an open mind, continual success will be within your grasp.

The First Step

"Step by Step and the thing is done!" Charles Atlas

We have all heard the age-old mantra that says, "Every journey begins with the first step." This is no different with success. However, what does that phrase mean? What is the first step you need to take in order to be successful? It is only prudent to define what the first step really is and figure out how to take it before we get into the process that is required to win consistently in your life. This first step is always the most challenging in any journey, physical or otherwise. However, we must take it in order to get anywhere at all. You would be amazed how fearful people are concerning taking this first step, no matter how big or small it may be. In fact, they could have everything they need to accomplish their desired tasks and yet still find some excuse never to bother moving forward.

Do not be one of those people who do not feel confident enough about their abilities to take even one single step towards what they were destined to do. Their doubts are well rooted in their minds, sowing seeds of fear and perceived weakness into their hearts. However, it is more than that. Upon a deeper look, they do not even know how to take that first step towards owning their own business, being certified in a new trade, or becoming a better, more supportive spouse. They may know they need to, but the actual doing—the process of putting one foot in front of the other in their journey—is just too insurmountable and overwhelming for them.

I liken it to learning how to walk as an infant. An infant does not simply get up and start walking all at once. Understandably, this process takes time and needs months to perfect. The young child must develop the muscles and the balance needed to hold them up in a standing position. Only after they have mastered the art of standing up can they take their first meaningful step. This step is taken with the support and guidance of their parents, often by holding their hands and drawing them out to make that step. In this process of taking the first step, they fall. A lot. In their determination to experience this new thing, these little ones try again, every single day, until they are able to take their first step on their own. Then, after the first step, they take another, and another and another, until they have finally mastered the art of walking.

In principle, it is the same with success. You must prepare yourself for whatever goals you desire to accomplish. This takes careful planning, research, and trial runs. Once you are able to stand on your own two feet, you must take the first step towards accomplishing those goals. You will make mistakes and sometimes it will seem as though you are going nowhere or, at times, even backward. It is at this moment that you must determine to continue pressing forward and with the proper drive, and you will start taking more steps forward than backward. Each step forward is a step closer to success, no matter how small it is. Finally, you will get to the point where you do not even think about taking steps; you will just walk and eventually run towards success without much consideration or effort at all.

The following are some important factors to consider as you prepare to take the first step towards success. The chances of failure greatly increase without a strong foundation. Consider these factors as your first step towards starting your journey.

Defining Success

"Any definition of success should be personal because it's so transitory. It's about shaping my own destiny." Anita Roddick

What exactly is success? How is it defined and what does it constitute? How do you even know when you have achieved it? In light of these questions, it makes sense to examine what we are actually attempting to do—establish what success is. Think about this: If you were a homebuilder, you could easily build a gorgeous house full of modern design and wonder, but what if your buyer was looking for a simple log cabin? It is crucial to have a clear understanding of what success is; otherwise you may never reach your intended target, goal, or dream.

Unfortunately, because it is subjective, it is difficult for everyone to have the same definition of success. Even dictionaries have various definitions of what success is. In fact, Dictionary.com defines success in four main ways:

1. The favorable or prosperous termination of attempts or endeavors.

2. The attainment of wealth, position, honors, or the like.

3. A successful performance or achievement.

4. A person or thing that is successful.

In truth, everyone should attempt to define their own success the best way they can. In your definition, you should be as thorough as possible, incorporating every minor detail and leaving nothing to chance. You need to be deliberate in your definition of success. What do you see when you visualize your place of success? What would your world look like if your dream were ever realized? How would others respond? All of these questions should be thoughtfully considered as you come up with your picture of success. The method is not as important as the level of detail. This enables you to see the reality of where you want your first step to take you.

In addition, you must be cautious not to get caught up in other people's success, or to have other people define your success for you, as this will almost certainly result in misery and/or failure. It is for this reason that you must create your own definition of success that incorporates your own dreams. You need to have a clear view of what you consider success before setting out to accomplish something awe-inspiring. Think of it like wearing the wrong-sized shoes while running a marathon. If you wear a pair of shoes that are a size too small, a couple of miles into the race and your feet will swell and cramp tremendously! If you wear a pair of shoes that are a size or two bigger, I foresee a journey filled with blisters, bruises, and rolled (if not sprained) ankles before you limp and trip your way to the finish line. No, only the right-sized shoes will do. Only they can offer the comfort and traction needed to see you through to the end of the marathon.

This is no different with your journey toward success. Just as the right-sized shoes will get you to the finish line faster and easier, the right-sized dream, tailored to fit you, will get you to your place of success. You must stay in your own lane, use the skills that were afforded to you, and pursue the opportunities and passions that you enjoy if you plan to achieve any level of fulfillment, happiness, or commitment to your goals and dreams. Without this, you will surely become discouraged and ultimately quit.

POSSESS YOUR SUCCESS: MASTERING THE LIMITLESS SUCESS METHOD

Dreams, Goals, Whys, and Hows

"A dream doesn't become reality through magic; it takes sweat, determination, and hard work." Colin Powell

We have all heard Dr. Martin Luther King Jr.'s renowned "I Have a Dream" speech that he brilliantly delivered in front of the Lincoln Memorial in Washington, D.C. back in 1963. This powerful speech took place in front of thousands of spectators. Dr. King, with great poise, discussed the current state of affairs of the nation concerning segregation, equality, and, above all else, freedom. But it was the vivid account of his dream that made his speech so legendary and memorable. In the great doctor's dream, all types of people could live together in harmony and happiness, liberated from the tyranny of prejudice and hate. Segregation would be defeated, and the very freedoms that this great nation was built upon would ring true for every citizen, in every citizen, and by every citizen.

As powerful as it was, Dr. King's dream was much more than that. His dream was a vision, a glimpse into a possible future. When we dream, we see what is not yet in existence. When we dream, we stare into something that, with the proper focus and diligence, can become a reality. When we dream, all things become possible. However, we have to work consciously towards making our dreams real. Otherwise, they are simply thoughts that drift along in our consciousness and soon fade away as more pressing, immediate items fight and demand for our undivided attention.

This is where goals come in. Some think that goals and dreams are one in the same. I disagree with that school of thought. A goal is in fact the very tool that makes a dream a reality. When we set goals, we are able to establish tangible milestones to realize our dreams. Otherwise, our dreams will certainly die. This is because our emotional, irrational psyches as humans make it difficult for us to stay focused on a given effort without the proper structure. That is just the way we are all wired. Setting goals keeps us focused and makes our dreams much more specific and reachable.

For instance, let us say you are an avid inventor who wants to build the next big thing in electronics. You passionately want a game-changer that will be used in every home worldwide, like an iPhone or a DVR. You envision people using your product on a daily basis or delivering speeches on a stage like Steve Jobs to droves of loyal enthusiasts and reporters. What I just described is more than a dream; it is a vision for your future as an inventor. Once you have your vision firmly planted in your mind, you must then set specific objectives on how to get there. The first goal would be to identify a problem that many people have that can be solved with technology. The next goal would be to devise and design an invention that would solve this problem. Another goal would be to determine the cost to produce the gadget. Each of these goals propels you to the next one, until you finally realize your dream and your vision becomes reality. Each one must be accomplished step by step.

The reason why I place such an emphasis on the distinction between a goal and a dream is that people have fantastic and achievable dreams every day. However, many of these same people do not actually see them to fruition. Why does this happen? Is it because they are too lazy, or because they have too much going on, or because they do not have the financial resources to do so? Perhaps. Either way, the underlying root cause is likely one of two things:

People have not made their "why," or their purpose, big enough.

People have not set the proper goals for themselves.

POSSESS YOUR SUCCESS: MASTERING THE LIMITLESS SUCESS METHOD

Most people are so focused on the second point that they become overwhelmed and flooded with self-doubt. It is immensely discouraging to have a huge dream and no clue as to how to achieve it. Less-motivated individuals will simply follow conventional wisdom, and if that does not work, they quit.

On the other hand, those who are bound for success use their "why" as motivation to figure out their "how." Once opportunities for success begin to appear, they set goals for themselves that are aligned with the bigger picture. The successful understand that if their "why" is bigger than their "how," the "how" will take care of itself. It will take some perseverance, effort, and creativity, but your reason for achieving your dream will help you find the tools and resources to make your goals doable.

Small Goals, Big Dreams

"Most 'impossible' goals can be met simply by breaking them down into bite size chunks, writing them down, believing them, and then going full speed ahead as if they were routine." Don Lancaster

Tim David once said, "If you are ready for something, that means it's too small." It is natural to feel overwhelmed by the sheer thought of what it would take to make your dreams come true. Success can be a very uncomfortable journey full of unknowns and failures. If you are at the beginning stages and want to increase your confidence with small wins, then set small, sooner achievable goals.

For instance, let us take Angie, an ambitious private college graduate who envisions fighting her way out of debt and achieving financial freedom. Unfortunately, she finds herself weighed down by:

Over $80,000 in student loan debt (6.8% APR)

$18,000 auto loan (5.6% APR)

$2,000 in credit card debt (18% APR).

Angie has a $2,000 head start from a work bonus she received. While it is possible eventually to pay off $100,000 in debt, it will still be a challenge given that she makes only $40,000 per year.

She can go about doing so in a few different ways. Being an ambitious person, she might try to pay off her biggest debt first to get it out of the way. Alternatively, Angie can pay off her highest interest rate loans first in an effort to save money in the end. However, according to Dave Ramsey's Debt Snowball strategy, these strategies will likely result in discouragement and ultimately abandonment of her goal.

I would highly recommend to Angie the Debt Snowball strategy, which works by paying off the smallest debts first and applying the freed-up cash flow to pay off the bigger debts. Again, as humans we are highly prone to emotional shifts, ebbs, and flows that often influence the choices we make. Like Angie, we may think that paying off the largest debts first may result in a higher degree of satisfaction in the end. We may also think that paying off her highest interest debts first may result in more saved money. However, the small wins gained by paying off the smallest debts will feed her motivation and keep her committed to her goal.

In the above scenario, Angie has a big dream that few people ever achieve. However, her strategy has a major bearing on the likelihood of her realizing that dream. The $2,000 credit card bill paid with her bonus (100% paid off) feels like a much bigger win than $2,000 paid on an $18,000 car loan (11% paid off) or $2,000 paid on a $80,000 student loan (2.5% paid off). This is not taking into consideration the interest she will have to pay on those loans. Remember, the small wins earn the big victories.

Start with the end in mind

"If you do not know where you are going, you will end up some place else." Yogi Berra

As your dreams and overall vision come together in your mind, you will begin to encounter opportunities to achieve them. Unfortunately, taking advantage of these opportunities is often much harder than originally thought, and soon you may find yourself right where you originally started, with nothing to show for it but wasted time and energy. If you constantly find yourself in this position, you are not alone; many desire greatness in their respective areas, but few actually get there.

To figure out why this happens, I would like to introduce a concept called "Structural Dynamics," originally developed by Robert Fritz, an established author and organizational consultant for some of the largest companies in the world. I interviewed one of his key understudies, marketing and branding expert Joel Alpert, on this very subject.

"When you try to create results in your life, it is vital to have perspective about what you want, what you have, and how to resolve this discrepancy," he explained. "Think of this discrepancy as a stretched-out rubber band. As you stretch the rubber band, you now have two points: one represents your goal, and the other represents your current reality. Your goal is the desired result, the thing you want to create. The current reality is where you are at in relationship to that goal.

"As you move towards your goal, the tension in the rubber band lessens. This dynamic is simple and straightforward. When you move from where you are to where you want to be, 'unstretching' (resolving) the discrepancy in the rubber band, you have just created your goal. Now there is no difference between these two points; you now have what you want." Essentially, when you move from your current reality to your goal, you enter a "resolving pattern;" you resolve the tension in your life just as you would the rubber band in Joel's example.

On the other hand, what happens to most of us during the journey is that distractions, doubts, and failures cause resistance to our intentions, bringing us back to the starting point. Joel adds, "Imagine there is one rubber band that's around your waist and is attached to the wall in front of you. In this example, as you move towards your goal, the stretch on that rubber band starts to dissipate, and you would achieve your goal if you got to that point. But you don't get to that point because there is a second rubber band at play." This is what is known as an "oscillating pattern," pulling you back and forth between your current reality and your goal. "In an oscillating pattern," he continues, "there is a second rubber band attached to your waist to the wall behind you. This rubber band represents belief systems or factors that are in conflict with your goal. As you move towards your goal, the second rubber band becomes more stretched than the first.

"Then, as you get caught up in your belief system, you get pulled backwards. When the tension of the rubber band in front of you grows, which happens when you realize your goal is really important to you, you'll let yourself be jerked forward towards your goal again. This oscillating pattern is called 'Structural Conflict.' You can see it quite clearly, once you know it exists. By nature of the thinking process and dynamics that are in play, you're doomed to be pulled back and forth like a yo-yo."

The only way out of Structural Conflict is to FOCUS: "Follow One Course Until Success." Clearly define and follow your goals, adjust on the fly, and mercilessly apply the principles outlined in this book until you are free from that resisting rubber band. "Structural Conflict is not a standard resolving pattern where there is a straightforward goal, a starting point, and action steps," Joel concludes. "When you focus on a clear end result and a clear starting point—without the structural conflict—you can create what you want."

The Importance of a Mentor

"Mentoring is a brain to pick, an ear to listen, and a push in the right direction." John Crosby

Furthermore, when we embark on a journey that we have never been on before, it can at first feel overwhelming. It is often a process just to motivate ourselves to reach the end goal. We have built a plan on how to execute it, but we have no way to know for sure if it works. Fortunately, we can find ourselves mentors. Mentors are people who have gone on the journey before us and are invaluable in that they can help ensure that you are on the right track. With their experience, they can show you brand new opportunities you have never seen before. They can also warn you of possible pitfalls and dangers on the road ahead. They can become almost a parental figure in your life. Just as a parent is there to keep their children from falling, mentors will keep us moving forward and aid us when we stumble.

The role of a mentor is very challenging. They must find novel and creative ways to devote time to helping develop others while ensuring their ship stays afloat as well. It often requires a certain level of mastery and patience that most do not even possess. It also takes a giving, empathetic heart to pour so much into another. However, the benefits to providing mentorship opportunities are tenfold. First, as a mentor, they give back to those who need help, many times for the simple reason that they might remember the distinct difficulties, frustrations, and growing pains they experienced when they were in that position. Second, in teaching others, they reaffirm and reinforce the very principles they learned on their own path to success. Third, it ensures that they will leave a legacy of goodwill and experiences for future generations to enjoy. It is even possible that they will learn something new or different while they are instilling ideologies and tips in their mentees, so long as they keep an open mind and an open heart.

A mentor can certainly aid you on your first steps of the journey towards lasting prosperity. Not only can they help you in defining what that first step is, but they can provide guidance on how to take that first step as well. Over the years, they have likely developed relationships and connections to make your first step a much easier one. They also might be able to share with you some advice on how to avoid pitfalls they have experienced. If you are extremely fortunate, you might find a mentor that will support your dream financially. One or all of these advantages could be freely available to you if you choose the right mentor.

POSSESS YOUR SUCCESS: MASTERING THE LIMITLESS SUCESS METHOD

When you first connect with a positive mentor, you will quickly realize how much they really love to share their experiences and mistakes. Whether it is boasting (which happens on occasion) or merely providing examples of areas in which they are operating in, they thoroughly enjoy reflecting on the various conquests and odysseys life has taken them through. As the conversation continues, you will begin to discover nuggets of wisdom that you can use in your own life experiences. Asking the right questions about their experiences draws them in further as it tells them you are sincerely interested in what they have to say. If all goes well, by the time you are done you will have gained invaluable insights on many of your pressing concerns and questions.

When looking for a mentor, consider the following key qualities:

1. Respectability: Ask yourself, do I really respect this person enough to listen to their words of advice; do I admire this person enough to emulate their actions; have they built up enough credibility to qualify them as my mentor? Remember, you do not want just anyone as a mentor—you want the best.

2. Experience: Ask yourself, how have they performed in the past in their areas of expertise? Is this experience relevant to my goals? Many people pretend they are making big waves in their lives and the lives of others, but the truth is that they are nothing but talk. It is up to you to separate the "Talkers" from the "Doers".

3. Compatibility: Ask yourself, are they doing the things I would like to pursue; what other talents and skills do they have that I am in-

terested in; is their life something I would like to emulate; do they even have the time or desire to mentor me? The last thing you want to do is to waste your time and efforts pestering someone who does not intend to help you. You could better spend that time planning your next steps to success or finding someone else who will make themselves available to you.

4. Trust: Ask yourself, can I trust this person to lead me in the right direction; can I trust this person with my dreams; can I trust this person when I am feeling discouraged; can I trust this person not to take advantage of my naiveté for their own gain? Additionally, you need to ensure that they trust you well enough to share their experiences, as many times it requires them to reveal a layer of vulnerability that others could exploit. Without that trust, a long-term working relationship cannot be formed.

If you can find someone who embodies these four character traits, it will help you immensely in the end. If you can find two or three willing to help you in different areas, then you know you have hit gold. The goal is to learn from each of their experiences and avoid possible dangers that can derail you on your track towards personal achievement.

To that point, there is no good reason why you should not have multiple mentors in your life if you can find them. I wholeheartedly recommend at least three major influences if possible. As you can imagine, if these mentors are the hard-working, successful individuals they appear to be, they are also likely extremely busy. If you can tie them down for just an hour for lunch, coffee, or even a simple phone call to pick their brains and update them on your status, you have accomplished a lot. Having multiple mentors also offers a number of perspectives for you to dwell on. Many times, I have found that a different perspective on my situation will shine some light on which direction I need to turn next or what consideration I may have missed.

As a personal side note, I do my best to meet with at least one mentor each month. When I began doing this, it made becoming successful in my career, my finances, and my life in general that much simpler. Not only was I able to develop strong relationships with my mentors without burning them out, but I was able to validate my thoughts and ideas against other, different viewpoints. Their collective feedback allowed me to fine-tune my strategies for success in ways that were just not possible if I had gone it alone.

However, finding a strong mentor will not be easy. It will take a lot of searching and vetting to find one who will match your personality and see your true potential. Not everyone with a voice will speak positively into your life.

Mentors are a surefire way to accelerate the process to achieve success in your goals. It may be intimidating (and often humbling) at first, but after a few meetings, it can really open doors to paths you never knew existed. Without the foresight and wisdom of those who have been there before me, I would have never come close to reaching the goals I have somehow achieved over the course of my life. Go out there and find yourself a mentor. You will be glad you did.

PFF: Pay it Forward First

"Giving is the master key to success, in all applications of human life." Bryant McGill

The final section of this chapter is one of the most important tools to achieving the Limitless life: to Pay it Forward First (PFF) to those who need it. Without a doubt, your success will come much slower if you ignore this principle, and if you keep your success all to yourself, you will truly risk losing everything.

Plenty of self-help books emphasize the principle of paying it forward. What is always surprising to me, however, is that these books always seem to highlight this principle at the end as if it were an afterthought. Not in this book. I place it at the beginning because giving determines your success, not the other way around. PFF, when instilled earlier on, provides a multitude of benefits both to you and to others.

Let us begin with the obvious reason to PFF: to help others less fortunate than yourself. When you provide for others, you not only deliver them out of a bad situation, but you also help place them on a path to success. What you offer may not seem like much, but you never know the other person's situation. Today might have been that individual's last day on this earth, but because of your aid, they might have found some way to press forward. Moreover, maybe that person will be in a position later on to bless others, or even you, more than you blessed them. That is the power of PFF.

You should also incorporate PFF into your routine because that is what we were meant to do in life. Even the Bible emphasizes PFF when it states to "give and it shall be given unto you" (Luke 6:38). This is also what is often referred to as the Law of Reciprocity, and when you give, others feel the need to give back to you. Whether you believe in a Higher Power or not, you cannot argue with the fact that society only thrives when people contribute to each other's overall welfare. Back in our early beginnings, our species realized that in order to survive, we must stick together and protect each other. When we give unselfishly, we feed our internal instincts to advance further society.

Another major reason to spread the wealth early on is a concept one of my financial mentors wisely, if not inappropriately, explained to me. Although unsavory in nature, the point is undoubtedly clear. When you eat a lot of food and there is no "release" of the excess, it could make you extremely sick inside and could even kill you! A similar situation occurs when giving is minimal—in essence, financial constipation.

A person without the practice of PFF might become selfish, opting to elevate themselves above others. This will result in isolation from their family, friends, and those around them, as their value to others decreases. As the bank account continues to grow, symptoms like paranoia, distrust, bitterness, depression, and fear begin to take hold. These mindsets can develop into mental and physical illnesses, resulting in a life no one would ever choose to live. PFF instills a habit of giving early and often, ensuring your focus is on others rather than yourself.

Have you ever noticed the giving patterns of the uber-successful, of people like Oprah, Bill Gates, and Bono? These are overwhelmingly huge givers! Philanthropy is in their DNA, and they are able to change the world because of it. There seems to be a strong correlation between giving and success; the more you give, the more likely you are to succeed. It humbles you by shifting the spotlight onto others. It also makes you a person of value, and people with a perceived high value naturally become successful by providing that value to others.

Of course, not everyone has the financial means to give at the moment, and that is okay. If you find yourself in that position, do not let that stop you. Give the little bit that you can, or find other ways to give. Volunteer your time at a shelter. Provide your gifts and services pro bono. Donate clothing or blood. Mentor others if you have the chance. PFF will make you more appreciative of what you have with the added benefits of blessing others and bolstering your faith to survive on less.

These are the first steps you must take to become successful in anything you do. You must define your success, seek out those who have experienced that type of success for advice and mentorship, set small goals with the end in mind, and give first. Of course, there will be many more lessons to learn, including how to master fear and failure, but now you have a firm foundation behind you to get started on your path to Limitless success.

Failing to Succeed

"When we give ourselves permission to fail, we at the same time give ourselves permission to excel." **Eloise Ristad**

In order to actually begin making your dreams a reality, we must discuss a few additional key points. You must declare yourself ready and willing to endure the pains and frustrations that come along with success. You must be able to stay strong and faithful, even when you do not feel like it. Moreover, you must embrace failure. Yes, what you are reading is correct: you must make failure your friend.

At this point, you might be a bit skeptical, even nervous, perhaps. You might be thinking, "Wait, I'm going to have to fail? I thought this was a 'success' book!" I would not blame you for feeling this way. This *is* a success book. Nonetheless, one factor everyone has to understand is that success is a journey, and although failures may seem to be obstacles, they are in reality merely stepping-stones on your long, arduous path to success. This is not to scare you, but to warn you of what you should expect when you say, "I desire to be successful in _____." In other words, you must *fail to succeed*. I know it sounds complex, but as you continue reading this chapter, things will begin to make more sense. Failure is defined in the Oxford Dictionary as the lack of success, and it is logical that no one ever desires a lack of success in his or her life. Even some supposedly "independent" scientists attempt to avoid failure when possible in their quest to find out what works and what does not, reports Manuella Adrian in her article on *Addictions Interventions*

Outcomes. She explains that many actually shy away from reporting studies that display any failure on how to treat addicts, even though it is equally as important to know what *does not* work and why, as it is knowing what *does* work and why. In reporting their negative findings, these researchers could dispel long held status quo beliefs about ineffective addiction intervention strategies. However, the stigma of failure is too much for some, opting rather to underreport their findings.

One of the most impactful failure statements that I have ever heard was quite surprisingly made in the animated movie *Meet the Robinsons*. In the film, the young protagonist, Lewis, is a genius inventor who, with the help of the mysterious Wilbur Robinson, an older boy from the future, is tasked to time travel to prevent the devious Bowler Hat Guy from ruining the past. Once they arrive in the future, however, they wind up crash-landing in their time machine. As Lewis's frustration rises after his failed attempts to fix the craft, Wilbur constantly repeats the phrase "Keep moving forward." The annoyed Lewis asks what he's talking about, to which Wilbur explains the motto that his dad, the original inventor of the time machine, swears by. In the future, his dad invents all kinds of gizmos, from the immensely useful to the insanely outlandish, and everything in between. During the course of the inception of the time machine, Wilbur's dad fails at least 952 times (he has the wreckage to prove it) before he finally gets it right. Nevertheless, he does not stop there. He continues working until he gets it right the second time, building an even better model than the first.

Yes, this is a fictional children's tale, but just imagine how many times Thomas Edison failed before he invented the light bulb, or how many times Alexander Graham Bell failed before he created the telephone, or how many times Steve Jobs failed before the dawn of the iPod. All they had to do was keep at it and get it right one time. One time and their names were then etched into history. When you are successful that one time, you will gain the confidence to be successful again, and again, and again.

Another brilliant moment in the movie happens during a scene when the Robinson family is enjoying dinner. After the first course, their robotic assistant Carl is about to serve up some delicious toasted peanut butter and jelly sandwiches with his handy PB&J gun when the darn thing jams (no pun intended). After much prodding and pleading, Lewis finally accepts the challenge of fixing it. Finally, he seems to have finished the repairs, but as Carl attempts to fire the gun again, it winds up uncontrollably dousing everyone in a huge peanut-butter-and-jelly-filled mess.

Everyone silently stares at each other with their mouths agape. However, instead of reprimanding him for the mess, they take the bewildered Lewis and congratulate him as if he had just won a Nobel Prize! Suddenly, with full bravado and fanfare, they proudly chant and display that most virtuous phrase: "Keep Moving Forward." Thus, instead of only looking at his failure, they see his failure as a means for him to become successful in the future. "From failing, you learn," they explain. "From success, not so much." You see, the child needed to understand that he was actually failing to succeed, and not just failing in and of itself.

If you prefer a real-life example, let us examine the story of Christopher Gardner, the real-life inspiration for the movie The Pursuit of Happyness. Gardner was brought up as a child of many unfortunate and ill-fated circumstances, including extreme poverty, domestic violence, and sexual abuse. His passion for finance led him to aspire to become a big shot on Wall Street, a possible way out of his deplorable situation for him and his son, Chris Gardner Jr.

ANDREW G. MCDONALD

Although he was extremely intelligent, he had not earned any educational degrees outside of a high school diploma. However, he did not let this stop him. His wife, sick of the constant disappointments and unable to cope with the realities of poverty, left him. This did not hold him back either. He and his son even ended up homeless and living on the street. It was merely a small setback for him, because during this time, Gardner was chasing his Wall Street dream. He earned his spot in Dean Witter Reynolds's trainee program, and although his wages were nothing short of paltry, he saw it as an opportunity. With each failure he encountered, he learned and grew. He let these failures become fuel to motivate him to continue moving forward.

While it is very true that you can look at his life up until this moment and point out that he has been a failure as a husband, a father, and even a man, you would be missing the point that he was really failing to succeed. Once he completed this training, he took off. He became a top earner at Bear Sterns & Co. He opened up his own brokerage firm. He wrote books and an autobiography. He started his own non-profit organizations. He now travels the globe delivering motivational speeches for large audiences. I will put it this way: when someone wants to make a movie about your life, you know you are a pretty big deal.

Again, I repeat: no one wants to fail. Failure does not feel good. People normally do not get excited about failure, and in some cultures, it could even lead to shame and bad omens for the entire family. Failure hurts your pride and dampens your confidence, and no one remembers those who failed completely in their quest to attain their goals and dreams. Do you think Chris enjoyed losing everything and struggling to keep himself and his son afloat? Likely not, but he found a way to make failure his friend. Failure is a necessary and valuable experience which, if used the right way, will make you better for it. Everyone has one time or other heard the famous quote "Whatever doesn't kill you only makes you stronger." This is especially true in failure, and without it, you will never learn to be successful.

This point also applies when it comes to proper exercise. Bodybuilders and health professionals alike have known about this for decades, and it can be directly applied to overall success, not just your fitness goals. The physiology of working out goes something like this: when you exercise a muscle group, you are literally tearing apart and breaking down muscles in your body. If you exercise that particular group long enough, it will eventually become fatigued; your muscles have failed. At this stage, it is recommended that you "feed" your muscles with protein and rest them. Over time, those muscles begin to heal and are able to withstand more and more punishment over an extended period. To sum it up, your muscles must experience complete failure before they can learn (via muscle memory) and grow (via muscle recovery). Without the continual punishment and pain, your muscles will never get stronger; in fact, they will atrophy and grow weaker, causing all sorts of other health problems for you.

The same can be said of the relationship between you and success. If you plan to be ultimately successful, you will need to experience failure. Just as your muscles need to experience pain, pressure, and failure to grow and become stronger, you must experience the same in order to learn and become successful in a given area. It will take a good amount of practice and repetition, but if you can gain something, even a small nugget of knowledge from each failure that you can use on your next try, success will naturally gravitate towards you.

One concept that was explained to me early on was to fail quickly and often. This way, the stakes are lower and you can afford to slip up. However, at the time, I did not understand the true meaning behind this statement. Why would I want to fail in my initial stages of an endeavor, let alone with frequency? Am I not likely to wind up discouraged and frustrated enough to quit? Well, the short answer is yes, if you do not truly have a desire to develop the mastery that you need to succeed. When you do not enjoy what you are doing, it will be easy to pack up and quit. However, in the things that you do enjoy doing or have a passion for, I can assure you that quitting is not so simple.

Case in point: When I was a sophomore in high school, I bravely decided to try out for the wrestling team. Actually, it was more because Ryan, one of my good friends at the time, pressured me into it. He had been wrestling for a year now, and he was obsessed with it. Anyone who disagreed that wrestling was great was nothing but a wimp. So, to save face and appear macho, and after weeks of constant prodding and ribbing, I reluctantly accepted his challenge. I had no idea the amount of hell that I was about to experience.

By the time I decided to check it out, the wrestling team was well into their conditioning phase. Boy was I in for a rude awakening! Two miles of track running and a mile of stadium running were in store for me every day at the very least—and that was just the warm up! Never mind the other core and cardio exercises I had to do to increase my conditioning or the actual practicing to learn each new move or technique. Practices dragged on and I felt like quitting constantly. The worst part about it was that I was not even good!

POSSESS YOUR SUCCESS: MASTERING THE LIMITLESS SUCESS METHOD

I never won any varsity- qualifying match, and the one time I even wrestled varsity level was when my fellow varsity counterpart was injured. Unfortunately, the opponent I faced in that match just so happened to be the best grappler in the state for that weight class and, as you can imagine, that experience did not end well for me.

So yes, I failed early and often, and it hurt. A lot. In fact, after that season, I decided to retire altogether from wrestling. However, I gained some experience and insights that I would then use throughout my life. First, I learned about how to condition my body and become diligent in physical fitness. I also learned about leadership and developed valuable team-building skills. Furthermore, I learned what I did not like. I finally understood that I could, instead of just participating because I was afraid of ridicule, simply quit wrestling, and move on to much more enjoyable pastimes in which I wanted to develop mastery. Most importantly, I learned how to persevere even in the face of constant failure. Although I wanted to quit early on, I was determined to finish out the season no matter how many times I failed. Yes, it was a challenging ordeal, but I knew that I could use these lessons in more than just wrestling.

Now, let me explain what happens when you fail at something you do have an interest in or a passion for: in my case, music. My love for music came before I could remember: even as a toddler, I could be seen banging away on my toy xylophone. My instrument of choice was the trumpet, and I had practiced diligently to become better every day. Unfortunately, I quickly realized that I was not one of the virtuosos that seemingly picked up an instrument and within a week was churning out concertos. As with many of the other pastimes in my life, I had to pour in my blood, sweat, and tears in order to see any form of improvement.

ANDREW G. MCDONALD

I was even more disadvantaged because I could not afford private lessons, and in middle school, I was assigned to one of the less fortunate schools in the city. In fact, I did not learn much about music theory or technique, and out of the 12 major scales, I barely knew one. Imagine my surprise when I finally found out in high school there were 11 more scales for me to learn, and that most of the other students already knew six of them, if not more! It seemed I was all but set up for failure in my musical career.

Throughout high school, I failed at getting solos, at multiple band leadership and honors band tryouts, and even in my own personal music goals. It was as if the other students were always a step ahead, and I would constantly have to redouble my efforts just to keep up. Instead of practicing one hour a day, I would need to practice two. I would spend my high school lunch breaks (and other class periods, if my teachers would let me) studiously learning and honing my trumpet skills. I just knew that I had the potential to be a phenomenal musician, and that if I only tried hard enough, I could be successful in that goal.

Nevertheless, while I did improve, I never became the principal trumpet player I envisioned myself to be in high school. In fact, out of 12 trumpet players in the premier high school band ensemble during my senior year, I was the third chair player—behind a freshman and a sophomore! Now, I will be honest: these underclassmen were awesome trumpet players and fully deserved their placing, and for a kid who three years prior only knew one scale, the third chair in the top-tier band was an amazing accomplishment. However, could you imagine the frustration and disappointment I felt simply because no matter how hard I tried, how many hours I had put in, or how many materials I studied, that I could not come close to the raw talent they had?

POSSESS YOUR SUCCESS: MASTERING THE LIMITLESS SUCESS METHOD

What was interesting was that, given all of the frustrations, failures, and defeats I experienced, I never quit playing. Instead of caving in and allowing my passion to fall by the wayside, I developed a work ethic that far surpasses most of the people I know. Today, I am one of the few of my high school friends that actually pick up their horn on a consistent basis. Every failure during that time motivated me to do better the next time. Every defeat humbled me and forced me to approach my weaknesses at a different angle. Now, because of the sheer number of times I tasted it early on, failure no longer scares me; it excites me and challenges me to press on in spite of its looming presence.

See, the persistently successful people recognize that they must learn how to fail gracefully; that is, learning how to move forward after a failure. It may seem counterintuitive at first—in effect, what they are doing is becoming really, really good at failing. It is vital that we lose our fear of failure and understand its role in our development or it will keep us from eventually becoming successful later on. In fact, I do not even call failures "failures" anymore; I call them "learning opportunities," taking the sting out of such an unfortunate outcome and flipping it on its head. Now I can use this learning opportunity to dust myself off, reflect, and try again.

A great way to become more comfortable with the idea of failure is by trying new things in a low-risk setting, such as cooking. The worse you think you are at it, the better. Set a goal to practice cooking 10 times in 30 days, regardless of how "unsavory" the results are. You may not become Julia Child or Bobby Flay, and that is fine. You may not even improve one bit. The key is to get comfortable with the idea of failure in order to reduce the sting of failing in higher-stakes scenarios. The less painful failure becomes, the less afraid of it you will be.

Therefore, in summary, failure is not something to be avoided; in all actuality, it should be embraced. All of the greats know this and do so every day. For them, there is a real chance every day that they may fail, just as there is a real chance they may be hit by a bus, struck by lightning, or encounter some other negative risk. Yet they continue to do what they were meant to do, even if it means failing a few times. Remember this: you can fail any number of times in life, but in all actuality, you only need to succeed once. That is the essence of "failing to succeed."

Fear's Bad Rap

"Fear is the brain's way of saying there is something important for you to overcome." Rachel Huber

Fear is one of the largest, most destructive enemies to success that you will ever encounter. It has a distracting, even paralyzing, effect that can absolutely derail anyone's goals and dreams. Fear is also a very human emotion that lies in waiting for the chance to rear its ugly head within all of us. Fear makes us question everything we want to do that is not routine and makes us anxious about the future. It also causes us to live in the past. Fear constantly has us looking at our mistakes, wondering helplessly how we could possibly do better given a spotty record of accomplishment. Fear has the same effect as a leech, sucking every ounce of enthusiasm and motivation right out of you until what is left is a withered and whimpering shell of a person. If left unchecked, fear will absolutely ruin your life. It spreads nothing but anxiety, doubt, and depression to those who succumb to it, and it soundly defeats anyone who attempts to eliminate it from their lives. I have not met a person yet that was not afraid of something. Am I being too harsh when it comes to fear? Does fear actually have a role to play in becoming successful in life? Should we embrace fear just as I have explained we should embrace failure? Where does fear even come from? In this chapter, I will explain my utter contempt for fear while also explaining its usefulness and purpose. Fear, like failure, is misrepresented and often misunderstood. Thus, I will attempt to demystify this unholy emotion. From this, you will truly gain an understanding of how fear works and thus weaken its stranglehold over your visions and dreams.

ANDREW G. MCDONALD

Fear is the Enemy... Or is It?

"Fear is a healthy instinct, not a sign of weakness. It is a natural self-defense mechanism that is common to felines, wolves, hyenas, and most humans." Hunter, S. Thomson

The definition of fear (from Oxford Dictionaries) states that it is "an unpleasant emotion caused by the belief that someone or something is dangerous, likely to cause pain, or a threat." That definition could not be any truer. When you fear something, you believe something bad is going to happen. Your blood pressure rises. You begin to sweat. Breathing becomes difficult. Your amygdala (the part of your brain that controls primal subconscious reactions) kicks your body into fight-or-flight mode, and in most instances when fear is introduced, you will want nothing more than to get away. Fear, in short, is the conditioned response to a threat: to run or fight.

Fundamentally, fear is the opposite of faith. In the Bible, faith is defined as "the substance of things hoped for, the evidence of things not seen" (Hebrews 11:1). If fear is the inverse, this means that fear is the substance of things that are worried about, and the evidence of things that are seen. Let us investigate a little deeper into this, because this statement has very significant implications. When we begin to let fear into our lives, we trust in what we see going on around us and worry about what might happen in the future. When you worry, you constantly think and speak outcomes that are related to your fears. As you will read in later chapters, your thoughts and words have substantial amounts of power over your life. This is why fear is so devastating to success; while faith empowers you to succeed, fear is the empowerment to fail.

POSSESS YOUR SUCCESS: MASTERING THE LIMITLESS SUCESS METHOD

Do you know what I believe to be the most persistent fear? It is one that is more persistent than the fear of death and is at the root of the fear of public speaking: the fear of failure. As I explained in the last chapter, no one likes to fail. However, countless people out there will not even attempt to achieve their ideal level of prosperity because they are so afraid of failing. In addition, no one is immune to this fear. The bravest of us, myself included, experience the fear of failure almost every day. Even when the stakes are as low as in video games, I have witnessed firsthand individuals that will quit and turn off the game rather than see the words "Game Over" or "You Failed." That type of negative feedback is just too much for them to overcome, and they will promptly exit before they experience the true sting of failure.

There was a time in my life when I hated fear. I wanted nothing to do with it and worked feverishly to eliminate it. I would take unnecessary risks just to overcome fear, even if the risk had no other benefit or value to me. To me, fear held people back far too much to be useful or important. Just think about how many times fear has held you back from doing something spectacular! How many times have you wanted to speak to someone you had a crush on, only to freeze every time at the thought of rejection? How many times have you turned down an opportunity to ask important questions in a meeting or classroom because you were afraid of what other people would think of you? How many times were you denied the realization of your vision, and you never gave yourself the chance to pick yourself up and try again, all because of fear? Yes, to me fear was nothing but a limiter.

However, over time, I began to realize that fear actually serves a very useful purpose in our lives, and it keeps us functioning as a society. Vanessa LoBue of Rutgers University explained that "fear is one of our most important emotions" as humans. Even though it seemed illogical that an emotion that often prevents us from development, achievement, and happiness could also be somehow useful, I knew there must be some reason that we have kept this primitive reaction within us for ages. Thus, I began to execute some much-needed research into the matter.

What I found may not shock many people, but is important to share nonetheless. Fear, just like many other primitive emotions, boils down to doing what it takes to survive in a conflict. As an example, allow me to introduce Caveman Joe. Caveman Joe is just that: a caveman. All this caveman wants to do is eat, sleep, and pass his chromosomes down to the next generation to ensure its survival. One day, while hunting and gathering, CJ runs into a large saber-toothed tiger den, complete with mother and cubs. The amygdala kicks in and CJ has two options: run or fight. The saber-toothed tiger is much bigger, faster, and stronger than he is, and Joe has no real weapons to stop such a formidable beast. Thus, the only logical action to take is to run as if his life depended on it, which in this case it surely does.

To keep Caveman Joe off the dinner menu, a decision needs to be made in milliseconds, and that is why the amygdala handles it. Another stone-aged example of fear safeguarding our survival lies in conformity. Early on, our ancestors realized that groups achieve far more than individuals on their own, and that teamwork is vital. While individuals can indeed survive on their own, societies provide an unparalleled level of safety and comfort and therefore a much better chance of survival than individuals do. However, to accomplish such a level of civility, our ancestors' physiologies needed a way to keep them conformed to society, and fear perfectly filled such a role. Because they so feared the risks of being alone without the protection of others, our ancestors had little choice but to conform. This is why we now seek approval from others and fear embarrassment: they are all just conformity and survival tactics from our ancestors.

What is truly interesting, however, is that we all share common fears, from early development stages to advanced age. Nearly all of us fear fierce and dangerous predators such as sharks, lions, and snakes. We also fear small, disease-carrying animals like roaches, rats, and spiders. These all come from survival instincts hard-wired into our psyche like the need for society. Many of us also share less rational fears, such as the fear of embarrassment, fear of confrontation, and fear of failure. Why do we still fear these outcomes? What makes them so frightening that some would rather fight a lion or catch a snake rather than face embarrassment, confrontation, or failure? How can we overcome seemingly irrational fears that have the potential to keep us from achieving what we were purposed to do on this earth?

First, I want to shed some light on the bad reputation that fear has. As I explained above, I used to believe that fear was a "bad" emotion that should be eliminated from your life. On the contrary, the absence of fear is ironically one of the scariest scenarios you can imagine. To illustrate my point, let us look at one of the deadliest shootings in the history of the United States: the Columbine High School attack. On April 20th, 1999, Eric Harris and Dylan Kiebold, two seniors at the school, felt it was appropriate to take the lives of 13 people, including one teacher and multiple students, while injuring more than 20 others on the school campus. Soon after the massacre, they took their own lives. They actually could have murdered even more people, seeing as they planned to bomb the school, which would have killed hundreds—but their homemade explosives never detonated.

ANDREW G. MCDONALD

If you look at these two cold-blooded murderers, they had everything they needed: the guns, the bombs, and the motive to kill people. Really, the one thing missing from them was fear. Throughout all of their prior years of suspected abuse and bullying, they lost their fear of hurting people; they lost their fear of consequences; they even lost their fear of death. In sum, they had no fear to hold them back from committing this lamented atrocity. If we lose fear, we could lose our notion of right and wrong. We could become unpredictable and easily cruel to one another. It would be a sad, sad world if we were to eliminate fear in our lives.

Fear also keeps us safe from harm. We are afraid of heights for a reason: If we were to fall from high enough, we could obviously die. When a gun is pointed at us, we surely enter into that fight-or-flight mode we developed over countless millennia. If someone were to lose their job, it makes sense for that person to fear that they cannot provide for their family. On the other hand, there is one powerful thing that fear does for us, as evidenced in the previous examples: Fear provides us with motivation. It gives us a reason to take action when we feel threatened. If we are atop a skyscraper and we get too close to the edge, our fear motivates us to move back to keep us from harm. Staring into the barrel of a gun motivates us to put our hands up to prevent a shooting. Being afraid of the consequences of unemployment spurs us to job-hunt vigorously. Fear keeps us going and actually keeps us strong and thriving as a society.

As you can see, fear really is not as bad as people make it out to be. The reputation for fear is that it makes you weak and ultimately holds you back from success. While that can be true, not all fear is harmful and, in many ways, it is healthy for your long-term future.

Instead of focusing on eliminating fear, we should pursue learning how to manage fear and begin using it to our advantage. If we can do this, we will never allow fear to take control of our lives again.

How to Manage and Control Fear

"I have to take control of fear and find a way to make it less frightening." Veronica Roth

As you take your first steps towards implementing the Limitless Success Method, you will begin to encounter new, unfamiliar territory and opportunities that require you to act in faith. There will also be difficult times and overwhelming circumstances that will arise and threaten to derail what you have sought to achieve. If you have ever built a sand castle too close to the water on the beach, you know what I mean. As soon as the castle begins to take shape, a wave suddenly comes ashore, threatening to destroy it. The key is to build a strong foundation of faith and understanding. It is much more effective to build a castle out of stone and rock than it is with sand and clay.

Two proven strategies to use on a continual basis to build such a foundation are rationalizing and simulating your fears. These are extremely useful practices in guarding against overwhelming or fear-paralyzing situations. The process is straightforward: When you encounter a situation where you begin to feel fear and anxiety irrationally taking over, simply ask yourself: "Why am I so afraid right now?" This question will engage the logical, more rational part of your brain, thereby keeping your emotions at bay. You are also defining your fear, making it more concrete and understandable. When your emotions get involved, you tend to overstate your circumstances out of panic. Small fears become large, looming clouds threatening to spew failure and doom in your life. Defining these concerns will help you bring them into perspective.

As you begin to answer the question, write down your concerns. No matter how major or minor your concerns are, they should all go down on paper. Again, you are attempting to engage your logical side, so writing things down will help calm you and give you time to think. It will also give you a sense of control and power over your fear. After that, write down on a separate sheet of paper ways to prevent this fear from happening, as well as steps to take if the fear were to materialize. In doing so, you begin reducing the chance of your fears actually being realized, and their impact if they do, thus making it much less terrifying for you. Once you have your two lists together, shred your list of fears with vigor. Burn it if you have to. It will be such a relief to rip apart your biggest fears! You will feel accomplished and relieved, as if you have vanquished a beast. This is all because you took the time to minimize the illogical aspects of fear and anxiety with actionable solutions.

As an illustration, let us say you were tasked to hold a commemoration speech in front of a large crowd. You, however, have always battled stage fright and performance anxiety. Even the mere thought of being up on stage with a captive audience staring at you makes you want to vomit and faint at the same time! What do you do? Well, according to the anti-fear strategies outlined above, you would want to begin with defining your fear. "What is the cause of my fears?" you ask. You may be afraid of tripping onstage as you walk towards the microphone. You may be afraid you will become flustered and forget your lines or lose your place. You may feel like you do not make a very good orator or speechwriter. You may even feel that everyone in the crowd will judge you while you give the speech. However, at the core of these issues are the fear of embarrassment and the confirmation of your negative perception of self-worth. You must next jot each of these fears down on a notepad or sheet of paper.

Now that you understand what you are dealing with in terms of fear and anxiety, you can begin to plan around them. How can one reduce the risk of tripping onstage? Obviously, by making sure your shoes are tied and picking up your feet when you walk, but also by ensuring you do not spend your focus or your breath on tripping in the first place. How can you avoid self-doubt and hiccups during your speech? By being well prepared and rehearsing often. How can you prevent people from judging you? It is not possible to do this, but you can limit yourself from thinking people are judging you, or simply prevent yourself from caring what people think about you.

You can also walk through some simulations on what would happen if your fears were realized. What would happen if you did trip? You could make a witty comment about it before you begin your speech, breaking the tension between yourself and the crowd. What if, in the delivery of the speech, you were not that good? That may just be your opinion; life will go on, and no one will likely think twice about any mistakes you made. On the upside, you can use this experience to say you faced a huge fear and made it through intact. What happens if people judge you? Who cares? People are going to judge you regardless of how well you perform, so do not let that stop you. In each case, you can find an opportunity to make the potential failure work for you and help you to become better in the future.

Now for the best part—shredding time! You can now destroy those fears (on paper and in real life) and focus on your preparation and contingency plans. As you work on this more and more, you will become more confident in yourself and find ways to move forward even in spite of fear, doubt, and uncertainty. Frightening circumstances will not affect you in the same way as they did before. You may still get nervous onstage, but you will be able to move past these feelings and use them to help you to deliver a masterful speech.

You can very clearly see that fear is not the evil monster you would expect in this case. Fear is only a warning for caution, and that is okay because it is something we all need in our lives. Sometimes it is good to pump the proverbial brakes a bit; it gives us pause and makes us think, "Is this really a good idea?" However, the trap we as humans fall into is allowing fear to take the keys, the wheel, and the gas pedal and completely steer us away from the direction we were meant to go. We allow it to take over our thoughts and affect our psyche. As time goes by, we begin to think that our fear is always right, even when God is telling us to move away from fear into faith.

You must learn how to use fear to your advantage and not let fear take advantage of you. This is easier said than done, but if you implement rationalization and simulation, you will have total dominion both over fear and the achievement of your goals.

Everything Begins with a Thought

"We are shaped by our thoughts; we become what we think."
Buddha

Everything begins with a thought, and it is amazing how powerful a single thought can be. The ancient and mysterious Egyptian pyramids, the lunar landing in 1969 that we Americans pride ourselves on, and even Cirque du Soleil—one of the most beautiful and awe-inspiring shows ever witnessed, all began with a singular thought. You cannot even lift a finger or roll your eyes without the microscopic firing of electrical impulses in your brain that represent conscious thinking. Go ahead, try it. Try to lift your finger without thinking about your finger, or without thinking about lifting, or without thinking at all. You will soon realize it is impossible to perform any of these effortless tasks without the power of a thought.

Now that you have done the necessary preparation and truly understand how fear and failure operate in your life, you may begin implementing the Limitless Success Method. The first step is to "Think It", with "it" being the success you defined in Chapter 2. No, I do not mean simply thinking about what success is, or thinking successfully, either. You can surely think about what success is until you are blue in the face, and you may not ever get up off the couch. You can also think successfully about anything. As long as you complete a coherent thought, congratulations! You have thought successfully. Not one of these tactics will translate into success on its own.

However, what I mean by Thinking It is to be completely success-minded. Everything you think about should be centered on success in your area of achievement or the steps needed to achieve success in that area. Negative thoughts about yourself should be completely defeated, as they serve no purpose on the path to success. In fact, as I will explain later, thinking and speaking negatively about yourself is like poisoning the water well—it is hazardous to everyone's health. You have to understand that the path to success begins with positivity, and positive thinking leads to positive doing.

When you Think It, you are thinking about the various strategies, methods, and requirements that you will need to become successful in a given endeavor. As stated in Chapter 2, start with the end in mind. What is the goal you wish to achieve? Next, you will need to take inventory of where you currently stand in regards to your goal and work from there. Review the tools and skills you have in your possession that can help you work towards your goals. Finally, identify the steps it will take to achieve that goal.

If your goal is to get to the next level in your career, what is it going to take? What skills do you have right now? What skills are needed for that next role? Do your skills match the skills needed for this role? Will you need to invest in training to develop those skills? Where will you get this training? Does your employer support upward movement, or are you going to have to look elsewhere? Is your resume sufficient, or will it require some professional networking with others to obtain the promotion? Will it take a moderate amount of networking, or will you have to become a networking socialite? And so forth.

Begin to write your thoughts down on paper. After a while, these thoughts will become goals and you will begin to form objectives around those goals. From there you will slowly begin to develop strategies to achieve those objectives. Eventually, what was once a collection of thoughts and questions will progress into a plan designed to achieve your goals and dreams. You can then use this plan as a springboard that will launch you into success, all because of a single thought about success in your career. Thoughts are really the inception of all things that can eventually become reality.

Hypochondriacs

"We are addicted to our thoughts. We cannot change anything if we cannot change our thinking." Santosh Kalwar

People just do not realize how potent thoughts can be. Even the belief that something is true, whether it is or not, can cause you to react as if it were. You may have heard of hypochondria, for example. Hypochondriacs are people who believe they have real illnesses, even though by any doctor's account, they are medically healthy. Nevertheless, it is more than that. They say they experience very real symptoms of their disease. From flu-like symptoms to numbness to even physical manifestations like internal bleeding, they look and play the part. However, every time they head to the doctor's office, they are either turned away with a clean bill of health or sent to a psychologist for a mental evaluation.

The worst part is that these hypochondriacs truly believe they are sick; it is almost insulting when they are told otherwise. Their belief is so strong that they convince their bodies to exhibit the very symptoms of their "disease." Anxiety grips them to the point that their rationale is completely switched off. Instead of relief when they hear that they are fine, they become even more anxious, even more suspicious. In short, they have fully convinced themselves and their bodies that they are sick, and anything else to the contrary is simply untrue. Even if you somehow convince the hypochondriac that their ailment is mental more than it is physical, they may still wonder if there is some physical component to their affliction, further feeding into their paranoia and anxiety.

Efforts to treat this disorder medically and psychologically have largely been in vain, unfortunately. As stated above, rationalizing with the patients is just not enough. They want to be told that their pain is real, because to them it is real. Sadly, this often leads to the frustration of both the doctors and their patients. However, doctors have been able to make some positive strides lately. Enter Dr. Ingvard Wilhelmsen of Bergen, Norway. He opened up a clinic to study these hypochondriac patients in an attempt to cure them of their perceived afflictions. Said Wilhelmsen: "They want to be seen in a hospital. So that's what I decided to do." With that, he opened up the Psychosomatic Clinic, the first hospital-based facility devoted to the treatment of severe health anxiety.

His research so far has shown that these criticized patients have deeper-rooted issues that cause their anxiety, such as depression or guilt for things said or done in their past. In truth, on some level they feel they deserve these imaginary illnesses and their psyche often causes their bodies to react in line with the symptoms of the illness. A stress migraine becomes a brain tumor. Nausea becomes Crohn's disease. A sneeze becomes full-blown pneumonia. Often their symptoms grow worse because of the anxiety and they really begin to make themselves ill, all because the psyche is telling the body to act in a certain way and the body listens.

This is how powerful the brain is. It is somehow able to trans-

POSSESS YOUR SUCCESS: MASTERING THE LIMITLESS SUCESS METHOD

form something that "isn't" into something that "is." All it takes is a thought, a dream, a suspicion, and things can manifest into reality. Fortunately, we can make the choice of what manifests and what does not by controlling our thoughts. With power and discipline over what we think, we can turn the impossible into the possible, or vice versa. All you have to do is transform a thought into a belief, and with the proper reinforcement, that belief will eventually become fact.

Here is proof of that: One of Wilhelmsen's first patients, Thor, battled with what to him was a sickness, something ranging between stomach ulcers and colon cancer. Thor was a happy-go-lucky 39-year-old enjoying life just as much as anyone else until, as he recalls, that one fateful day in 1989. Thor suddenly came down with a bad case of diarrhea, and his situation went downhill from there. According to him, he experienced cramping so severe that he could not go an hour without doubling over in pain, and it was so intense that he thought he could be dying of some terrible disease. He tried quitting his job, seeking professional medical advice, switching his diet on multiple occasions, and running a myriad of medical tests (all of which came back negative). Meanwhile, his symptoms were getting worse, to the point that he was even starting to see blood in his stool and fainting on some occasions. Once he began seeing Dr. Wilhelmsen, he began to see results—not due to a diagnosis or prescription but a change in Thor's perspective.

Wilhelmsen explained, "We try to find out whether the patient really misinterprets his or her bodily symptoms." This included identifying misconceptions about health, like thinking every symptom is the result of a more serious issue. In Thor's case, the doctor had him keep a journal to show him that his debilitating ailments always followed periods of extreme anxiety and thus proved his anxiety was the root cause of his problems. He still had doubts, and nevertheless continued to conjure up various maladies, but after a while, the worries about serious illnesses faded. "I have started to think about what I am thinking," said Thor. "When I feel anxious, I have learned to say, 'this has nothing to do with disease. You can cope with this.'"

Perspective

"We can complain because rose bushes have thorns or rejoice because thorns have rose bushes." Abraham Lincoln

You can see in Wilhelmsen's care plan that he encouraged Thor not to alter his condition, but his *perspective*. As stubborn as Thor was about his "sickness," Wilhelmsen took each complaint very seriously. He then used facts and exercises to help his patient make his own conclusions about the situation. Thinking on sickness produced sickness. However, when the perspective shifted from the physical realm to the mental one, real progress was made. Thus, in order to alter the circumstances around you, you must first learn to alter your perspective.

One thing that forms your perspective is your physiological being, your size, shape, brain capacity, and genes. These physical features are hardwired into your system and can be very difficult to change. For example, I am 5'7" and well past my growing stage. Sadly, at this point, there just have not been the technological and biological advances necessary to change my height more than a couple centimeters. Although there are other things such as weight and skin tone that I can change to a certain degree, I simply was not born with the genes to grow any taller, and I will likely shrink more than I will grow as I get older.

Being slightly below average in height has provided me with a much different perspective than a taller man. A man who is closer to 6'2" will probably be more desirable in the sports world, and is more likely to become a CEO of a company (yes, there is a proven correlation between height and career advancement in men!). Although I am athletic, intelligent, and a natural leader, taller men might still have a slight advantage over me. Taller women than I always seemed to date even taller men, leaving me to search for shorter women as potential mates. Taller women, on the other hand, will have a very different perspective. At young ages, many are teased for their above-average height. In what seems to be a trend, men prefer to date women that are their height or shorter, so they may have the opposite problem than I do. Although we are all humans, physical features such as our height and our sex will cause us to form many different opinions of ourselves, of other people, and of the world around us.

Another component of your perspective is your external environment. Everyone around you, the area you grew up in, and the places you have been throughout your life—these have all influenced you in one way or another. Many of those who were born and raised in the ghettos and slums of major urban areas never leave and are almost destined to spend the rest of their lives impoverished. Have you ever heard of the saying, "You can take a person out of the ghetto, but you can't take the ghetto out of a person?" Essentially, people's values are mostly derived from those around them, and it proves to be difficult to convince them to think outside of their worldview because it has been so ingrained into their very being.

These two components become monumental factors when you attribute them to success. Just think of the last time you had an argument or debate with someone who was unwilling to "see the other side." It was as if their ideas were truth and you could do nothing to change them. Talking and reasoning with them were simply exercises in futility. Their preconceived notions, their experience, and their upbringing have had such a profound effect on them that they feel it would be impossible for them to be wrong. Unfortunately, this is also the result for many when they perceive their ability to achieve goals and dreams. Their perspective, formed by their past, background, physical features, and their interactions with others, determine their path to success. If they could only view themselves more objectively and take more risks, they would astound themselves with the amount of success they might attain.

The Limited vs. the Limitless

"Our limitations and successes will be based, most often, on our own expectations for ourselves. What the mind dwells upon, the body acts upon." Dennis Waitley

These types of individuals, the ones who are limited by their past and other people's opinions, are said to have a "Limited" view of themselves. The Limited firmly believe that they have a set limit of ability to accomplish tasks, goals, and dreams, and anything else is essentially beyond their grasp. They are not likely to challenge themselves very much and they avoid risk as much as possible. Failure is their enemy, and they stick to what they are good at to mitigate risk. To the Limited, safety means more to them than the experiences necessary to develop a mastery or competence in a given subject area. They generally look for stability and control in their lives, settling for routines in lieu of spontaneity.

On the other hand, you have those with a "Limitless" view of themselves. The Limitless believe that with enough devotion, diligence, and discipline, they can achieve anything they set out to do. Their ability to succeed is solely linked to their imagination and drive. A challenge presents an opportunity to grow as they seek to develop a mastery over their subject areas. They encourage risk taking and welcome failure because they know that they can learn from their mistakes and prevent them in the future. In fact, they are always in search of new places to conquer and they fear mediocrity might lead to complacency. Like those with Limited worldviews, the Limitless also make use of routines and schedules, although these tools are used specifically for the development and realization of their goals and dreams instead of a means to gain some sense of control and safety in their lives.

When responding to a challenge, these two groups handle their circumstances differently. The Limited perform a simple calculation by measuring their ability against the requirements of the challenge. Furthermore, they evaluate the performance of others for validation of their own abilities. If they determine that they may lack the ability to complete the challenge, or that risks of failure outweigh the benefits of completing the challenge in any way, they throw their hands up in the air and admit defeat. For those with a Limitless view of themselves, the likelihood of completion of a difficult task does not depend on their perceived ability to do so. In essence, they are certain they will succeed in spite of how others fared in attempting the very same feats, even when they think the odds are stacked against them.

This was precisely demonstrated in an experiment conducted by

ANDREW G. MCDONALD

Thompson and Musket in 2005. Close to 100 college students were split into two groups between those with a Limited and Limitless view of personal ability and selected to participate in a variety of activities, including surveys and difficult puzzles. The puzzles were given in such a way that they either forced a participant to fail or to succeed (these puzzles were rigged no matter what the participants did) or simply gave them the *opportunity* to succeed (results were actually determined by the ability of the participant). The participants were then primed to either measure their performance against the performance of others (i.e. "I thought about how I was doing compared to others") or measure their performance without comparing their performance to the performance of others (i.e. "I felt satisfied because I was trying hard") by means of a survey. After they were primed, they were asked to complete additional puzzles (again some participants had rigged puzzles and some did not), and they were once more asked to complete a survey assessing their frame of mind while completing the second set of puzzles.

The results of the experiment were noteworthy. On the second set of puzzles, the students who had a Limited view of their abilities performed just as well as the Limitless when they were simply told to focus on their own performance. When they compared their results of the first set of puzzles to others, these very same Limited individuals actually performed worse than the Limitless when it was time to complete the second set of puzzles. For students who believed their abilities were Limitless, they performed at a high level regardless of whether they succeeded or failed. In fact, the only time their performance suffered in the second trial was when: 1) they generally failed in the first trial; and 2) they compared their results of the first trial to others.

POSSESS YOUR SUCCESS: MASTERING THE LIMITLESS SUCESS METHOD

So what does this have to do with success? Well, the first step to success, Thinking It, is hinged on two things: perspective and focus. Your perspective, as discussed before, can largely affect your ability to succeed in anything, even in conquering disabling thought patterns. Thompson and Musket's experiment proves that those with the perspective of Limitless success are in fact able to succeed whether they have failed in the past or not. For individuals that perceive they have limits, each failure most likely leads to negative emotions about themselves, reiterating their stance on their abilities and thus leading to more failures.

If you fall into the Limited category and are still looking to succeed, do not worry—there is still hope. You still have a chance to succeed, even in spite of your current perspective and past failures. However, you will have to perform one of two actions: change your perspective to a Limitless perspective, or concentrate on yourself and ignore how everyone else is doing. The latter is the essence of focus, which is the amount of concentration you place on a matter. Your focus sets the tone of a given situation. Those who tend to focus on problems seem to have more problems in their life, while those who focus on the solution tend to overcome their problems.

Let us take myself as an example. One of my far-out dreams as a kid was to become a football superstar. I imagined myself as a star running back, tearing apart defenses with my athleticism, lightning-fast speed, and agility. Once the lights were on me and I ran out onto the field in front of tens of thousands of screaming fans, I would shine! In reality, however, I would have been a short, scrawny football player, no matter which position I played. I was barely 5'7", and the heaviest I had ever weighed in high school was 135 pounds. Furthermore, I had an extremely demanding schedule as a kid with various competing priorities. In addition to the normal household duties and schoolwork, I was an active participant of the high school marching band, something that I was fiercely loyal to and very proficient at, as well as wrestled on the high school team at one point and took karate lessons. With all of these challenges to overcome, I stuck with what was familiar to me, never even giving the football dream a chance.

Do you see the problem with what I did? In this situation, I focused solely on my limitations. What would have happened if I had just tried out anyway? Who knows what I could have done with that chance. Although limited in quantity, there are some very successful running backs in college and even the NFL with my same height and weight challenges. Just look at NFL running back legend Barry Sanders and fellow running back Darren Sproles when they got their moment in the spotlight.

Barry Sanders

"Power knows the truth. It's speaking the truth to yourself that's the challenge."-Barry Sanders

Barry Sanders was one of the most prolific running backs to grace the sport of football. Electric with the ball in his hands, he played 10 seasons with the Detroit Lions and led the NFL in rushing four times. He was so successful that he was selected every year for the Pro Bowl, and on August 8, 2004, he was inducted into the Pro Football Hall of Fame.

However, that success did not come easily. Back in high school, Barry Sanders's small height (a measly 5'8") discouraged coaches from playing him at running back until the last five games of his senior year. To boot, he barely weighed 200 lbs. However, when he finally got the opportunity to shine, he did not disappoint, amassing an eye-popping 1,417 yards across those final five games! In 1988, Sanders became the starting halfback at Oklahoma State University and rushed for 2,628 yards, crushing the record for the best single season rushing performance in the history of the National Collegiate Athletic Association.

That year, Barry won the Heisman Trophy as the nation's best college football player. Sadly, there was trouble brewing at OSU, and the following year the university was put on probation. This prompted Sanders to declare himself eligible for the professional draft, where he was selected by the Detroit Lions as the third overall pick in the 1989 NFL draft.

He made his professional debut three days after signing with the Detroit Lions, and the rest, as they say, is history. In 1990, Barry Sanders topped all ground gainers with 1,304 yards rushing; he repeated this feat in 1994 with 1,883 yards and again in 1996 with 1,553 yards. The most rousing feat of his career, however, was in 1997 when he rushed 2,053 yards (league-best) and gained another 305 yards on 33 catches for an astonishing 2,358 combined yards gained. Never once did he let his height become a defining obstacle in his NFL career.

Darren Sproles

"I heard I was too small to play in high school, in college, in the NFL. It just made me work harder."-Darren Sproles

ANDREW G. MCDONALD

Another tiny man who made a huge impact on the league was Darren Sproles. Born in Waterloo, Iowa, Sproles played college football at Kansas State before beginning his professional career in the NFL with the San Diego Chargers. In his 9-year NFL career, Darren Sproles has played 138 games with a career total of 437 carries for 2,221 yards and 11 touchdowns while adding 378 receptions for 3,381 yards with 27 touchdowns.

Sproles faced challenges at every stage of his life, from youth football in Johnson County to his college days at Kansas State, all the way into his NFL career. Born to Larry and the late Annette Sproles, Darren never grew beyond 5'6" and 190 lbs., and in addition had a speech impediment that became a detriment to his confidence. However, even with his physical limitations, Darren got offers from various universities to play football. In the end, he chose Kansas State over others to stay close to his mother, who suffered from cancer. For him, his mother was his hero, the one who helped him focus on the right things.

Neither his small stature nor his adverse circumstances deterred him from making it big in college. From 2001 to 2004, he appeared in 45 games in total. He was also the team captain in both his junior and senior seasons and was named the team's Offensive MVP between 2003 and 2004. After being selected in the fourth round of the 2005 NFL Draft by the Chargers, he totaled 1,528 kickoff return yards in his first campaign. Disaster struck in 2006 when he missed the entire season recovering from a fractured ankle, but he came back energetically in 2007 to finish with a record-breaking 2,696 all-purpose yards.

POSSESS YOUR SUCCESS: MASTERING THE LIMITLESS SUCESS METHOD

Today, Sproles has established himself as one of the most dynamic players in the NFL circuit. He was acquired by the Philadelphia Eagles from the New Orleans Saints in 2014, four years after his last season with the Chargers. With 15,187 all-purpose yards, he is second only to Steve Smith Sr. in the all-time category. Although he has not quite enjoyed the success of Barry Sanders, he has still attained a decorated NFL career and currently serves as an inspiration to those suffering from a Limited mindset.

What were the differences between these star football players and myself? My perspective was that I could not be a serious football player. They tried anyway, knowing that they could. My focus was on how I was only 135 pounds. They ate more and worked out harder. I made excuses about the many different ways I was being pulled all the time. They had one goal: becoming the best football player they could possibly be. I had a Limited perspective and achieved nothing in that area because of it. They had a Limitless perspective and they achieved stardom.

The keys here are focus and perspective. That laser-eyed focus and your perspective on your circumstances are what will keep you from listening to the doubters around you as well as your own worst critic: yourself. It is difficult, if not impossible, to turn thoughts into action without these two abilities. Thinking you will make an 'A' on that test, meditating on that same thought repeatedly, will surely cause you to begin believing it! Barry Sanders and Darren Sproles thought they could play professionally, and their belief helped bring it to pass.

ANDREW G. MCDONALD

Visualizing Your Success

"Visualize things before you do them. It is like having a mental workshop." Jack Youngblood

The masters of success, the Limitless, often utilize what seems to be the greatest mind trick of all time to achieve their goals consistently: visualization. Visualization occurs when you not only think of the results of your actions, but you vividly experience the results in your mind. It is essentially the mental preparation for a given task and is to be used as a supplement to (and in some cases, in lieu of) actual physical practice.

You see, there are three main reasons why visualization can improve your chances of success. First, in your mind, you can simulate the correct method of performance. Ever heard of the phrase, "Perfect practice makes perfect"? Visualizing and rehearsing the steps in your head creates a way to achieve that "perfect practice." Second, your brain begins to make significant neurological connections similar to what takes place during actual practice. This helps you to remember what you have mentally rehearsed when it becomes time to implement. Third, visualization results in a huge confidence boost. When you mentally visualize the scenario, you not only see yourself taking the steps required to succeed, but you are also visualizing the result. Repeatedly visualizing your success makes you more comfortable with the overall process and more confident in your abilities to perform successfully when it counts.

Visualization is more than just thinking happy thoughts. It combines positive outcomes with positive processes to continue the preparation process even when no physical action is being taken. In a visualization session, it is best to begin by writing down the goal or goals you would like to achieve. Do not rely on your memory, as

POSSESS YOUR SUCCESS: MASTERING THE LIMITLESS SUCESS METHOD

it can become clouded and distracted at times. Once you have your goals written down, take a few deep breaths and begin imagining the situations in which you want to have success. Determine who is in the room or area around you, where you are placed, and your emotions at the time. You want to make this as intense an experience as possible, so spare no details. Your mission is to turn this collection of thoughts into a vivid memory, so narrow your attention all the way down to what you are wearing in your visualization.

After you have established the setting, turn your attention to the problem you are attempting to solve or the obstacle blocking your way. Also, reflect on the method that is going to be used to achieve victory. Maybe it is the speaking points that you will use to deliver a powerful message to your audience, or the modes of transportation it requires to get to the destinations of your dream vacation. All of these must be visualized to reinforce your confidence and drive, concentrating more on the solution than the problem. Otherwise, you run the risk of self-doubt and fear holding you back.

Now imagine you have just completed your goal. Envision the exhilarating joy of your success and the reaction of others to your accomplishment. Take things a step further and see the impact of your success on the world. If you have delivered a killer presentation, imagine the standing ovation you receive and your audience taking your message to heart. If you have just come back from your dream vacation, imagine reflecting on the photos and sharing them with others. The key is to meditate on the whole process from beginning to end and make it a distinct memory you can refer to later on. Continual visualization of these goals and dreams will then open up your eyes to opportunities that will turn them into tangible realities.

ANDREW G. MCDONALD

The ideal setting for visualization is a quiet, isolated place with minimal distractions. This allows for the best possible focus on your goals and visions. It is easy to say you are busy, but do not let your schedule discourage you from finding time to visualize. It is perfectly acceptable to visualize on your break at work or during your commute. I personally visualize while I am taking a shower or shaving. The main takeaway is to incorporate extra mental reps to supplement your actual attempts at success.

Now, I understand some readers will find this technique either dubious or unnecessary. However, studies have shown that mental rehearsal and visualization, when paired with actual practice, enhances skill and performance while also improving communication, education, and psychology. What is most interesting is that for years athletes have known about the power of visualization. In keeping with the football examples above, let us examine one of the best NFL catches of 2014, if not in NFL history.

On November 23, 2014, I was, like 20 million or so other Americans, lounging around the house watching Sunday Night Football. That night, the New York Giants had been playing the Dallas Cowboys, and it was set to be an exciting matchup. New York had recently lost their star wide receiver, Victor Cruz, to a season-ending knee injury, but their relatively unknown rookie replacement was showing some real promise.

On one fateful play during that game, everything was about to change for the rookie. Giants quarterback Eli Manning threw a bomb towards the end zone as the inexperienced receiver zoomed past the Dallas defender. Knowing he was beat, the defender grabbed onto the rookie in a last-ditch attempt to prevent a surefire touchdown. In response, the receiver leapt and arched backwards, stretched out one hand to secure the ball, and landed in the end zone for a touchdown. I was beside myself. What an acrobatic catch! I thought. I just have to see the replay of that grab. Upon further review, the catch was even more impressive that initially thought. The wide receiver did not use one hand; he managed to haul in that improbable touchdown catch with *only three fingers*. With that catch, the legend of wide receiver Odell Beckham Jr. had begun.

In his short professional career—he has only appeared in 15 games as of this writing—he has made some incredible catches, and in 2014 had the most successful rookie season in NFL history. When asked by NFL UP! How he makes such amazing plays, he attributes the visualization of his catches to a significant portion of his success. On his first day of practice, he recalls:

"I woke up and was like, 'I'm going to catch a ball today with one hand in practice. I remembered how it was in my dream, and the situation came up in practice and it was the same exact thing. Déjà vu."

The fact that he was able to see his catches before he made them calmed him down and made him much more confident in his abilities to perform at an elite level. Visualization worked for him and it can work for you, too.

A famous scripture from the Bible reads, "As he thinketh in his heart, so is he" (Proverbs 23:7). In both the spiritual as well as the practical sense, your thinking has a lot more to do with your success than you realize. The mere inception of a thought could possibly determine everything from your outlook on life to your body's

Thoughts are Seeds

"Dreams are the seeds of change. Nothing ever grows without a seed and nothing ever changes without a dream." **Debby Boone**

My wife and I moved into our first home last August. During the housing inspection, the inspector and I noticed a tiny plant growing on the side of my house. I asked him if we should get rid of it, mistaking it as a weed. "Actually," he said, "it's a cucumber plant. Seems one of the builders had a veggie sandwich for lunch and dropped a seed on the ground." The idea of it all astounded me. One small seed, whether intended or not, dropped onto the ground, established itself in fertile soil, and became a harvest-producing plant. All it took was the right conditions.

In the very same way, thoughts are seeds. A thought planted in your mind, as small and as insignificant as it may be, can take root, slowly growing from a sprout to a sapling until eventually, your thought has become a huge and towering tree, full of delicious, juicy fruit ripe for the picking. This fruit, after some time, will eventually fall to the ground, leaving behind even more seeds in the soil. At that point, the cycle continues and what was once an area of bare land over time becomes a large and expansive forest.

This is how successful people become successful in the first place; they plant their seeds in fertile soil. In the Bible, there are scores of references to planting and harvesting, and for good reason, too. Just like farmers sow their seed in expectation of a fruitful harvest, so too should we create thoughts that will take hold of and lead us to fruitful success in our lives. Of course, this also means that we will have to devote a lot of effort and time into tending to these fresh, young ideas. We must keep our dreams nourished and protect them from harmful elements. If they grow weak or begin sagging, we must prop them up. If they are growing too rapidly, we must prune and shape them. It may seem onerous and grueling at first, but over time, I promise you will see results.

"Sure," you might respond, "that's easy for you to say. However, how are you supposed to sow when you have no good seed? When you can barely keep it together because your spouse abuses you on a nightly basis? When your life has been filled with nothing but drugs and alcohol, and you are unable to think about anything else? When you are severely depressed, even contemplating suicide, and no one really understands what you are going through, or worse: no one cares enough to do anything about it?" Well, to answer those questions, we need to understand the biology of a weed.

It was a gorgeous 78 degrees on the first day of spring. You could feel the warmth of the sun radiating on your skin, and there was not a cloud in the sky. There was a light, gentle breeze, just enough for you to enjoy without urging you to button up. I was thoroughly appreciating the beautiful springtime weather, rolling down the windows to make the most out of an otherwise tedious commute home from work. Finally, as I made it home, I happened to glance at my garden and lawn. Hmmm, I thought, there are a couple of weeds attempting to invade. I should probably do something about that this weekend. I made a mental note and strolled on inside the house.

ANDREW G. MCDONALD

A couple of days later, I decided to inspect the grass again. I could not believe my eyes! Lo and behold, there were twice as many weeds as there were the other day! I said to myself, shoot! I am really going to have to take control of my lawn this spring or else I will be watering the weeds by the summer! By the time the weekend arrived, my lawn and garden were fully infested with weeds and crabgrass. They were everywhere. I hurried to the nearest home improvement store and bought the biggest container of weed-killer I could find. Too little, too late, unfortunately, because once weeds start establishing themselves, they will run rampant and are very difficult to stop.

This is the trouble with negative thoughts and emotions like doubt, fear, and anxiety; they are like weeds. They began as one or two small sprouts, and before you know it, they have completely dominated your mind, choking off the more desirable thoughts and feelings like dreams, goals, and ambitions from the necessary nourishment they so desperately need to survive. If left unchecked, these "weeds" will leave your mind uninhabitable.

It reminds me of my recent home-buying experience. You do not know how many times my wife and I passed on a beautiful, well-built home that had everything you could ask for in the pictures because of weed-ridden landscapes. Think of it like this: No one wants to live in or next to a house surrounded by weeds. In fact, even visiting homes in that type of condition leaves a bad taste in your mouth. The same is true of people who think negatively. No one wants to be that person, live with that person, or even be around that person. It is generally an unpleasant experience for everyone.

A sad reality for some is that they believe that they can actually think negatively and expect positive results in their life. This is ludicrous when you really break it down. Thoughts are seeds, and if you plant weeds, you should not expect oranges, bananas, or peaches to grow. It is impossible to produce anything from those weeds— except more weeds.

There are two types of weeds: yearly weeds like annuals and biennials, and perennial weeds that last several years. Yearly weeds reproduce using seeds and can span multiple generations before the year is over. Perennial weeds, on the other hand, establish long roots to entrench themselves in the ground, and as the roots grow and expand, so does the size and dominion of the weed. Both are difficult to get rid of. However, perennials are perhaps the greater of the two evils due to their long lifespan and resistance to death. You can treat the stalks and flowers all you like, but until you completely remove their root systems, you will always have a weed problem. Moreover, some annual and perennial weeds are actually considered noxious; they can be very aggressive in crowding out other, more desirable plants, and may even have high toxicity levels that can poison the plants and animals around it, causing the land to be unfertile.

Now, imagine your mind as the garden or lawn you are working so desperately to protect. The yearly weeds are the fleeting, repetitive thoughts you may experience from day to day, serving only to ruin your mood, your joy, or your confidence. They may be caused by a one-off circumstance or a string of frequent occurrences, such as getting into a spat with your significant other or having an awful day at work. "I'm terrible at this," you say to yourself as you inevitably think back to all of the previous mistakes you have made in this area. "Why does this keep happening? Why can't things just go smoothly for once?" You reason with yourself but it just does not seem to be working because your mental garden is being overrun by a never-ending advance of weeds. Try as you might, you slowly grow more and more worn out until you finally succumb to your negative thoughts. Exasperated, you exclaim "Maybe that's just who we are and things will never change!" In this respect, your negative thoughts and feelings can become so noxious that they may not only affect your goals and dreams, but also the goals and dreams of the people around you.

This is when the perennial weeds start to grow and take form. They become deep-rooted thoughts and feelings and, over time, they integrate into your personality. They start invading other parts of your mind and make you feel like nothing you can do will help. Your hopes and dreams wither, dry up, and eventually die off through lack of nutrients. Your fruitful excitement and optimism become barren depression and pessimism. It could take years and years to destroy these psychological weeds; one application of mental Round Up is just not going to cut it. I cannot overstate the devastation and despair these psychological pests can bring about. They must be mitigated and controlled before they start to deal some serious damage in your life.

Experts say the most effective method of the elimination of weeds is good ole prevention. This means treating your lawn before the weeds have a chance to grow. When applying this to your psyche, you must make sure your mind is set on success and build up your confidence levels. Whether this means reading up on marital issues and how to resolve them before you say "I do," or practicing and nurturing the required on-the-job skills before you even have an interview, these adjustments will go a long way towards developing the confidence necessary to withstand the assault of negative thoughts your life circumstances will cause. Remember, just as you will not be able to keep 100% of weeds from forming in your front yard, you will invariably form fleeting, negative thoughts from time to time. However, if you are diligent and focused, you can keep your weeds to a minimum and enjoy the healthy fruits of your labor.

Of course, prevention only works at a time when a lawn or garden is weed-free. Say, for instance, your mind has already fallen victim to the annual and perennial weeds and they have already taken root, affecting your mood, morale, or personality. Well, this is where things get a bit more challenging (not impossible, just challenging). Yes, it will take a lot more effort. It will most certainly require a particular level of devotion and diligence. To eliminate these weeds, you must be consistent in your weed-killing application. If you can simply remain consistent and focused, you will find that your mental weeds will begin to die off, freeing you from the bondage of negativity and doubt. This is the perfect time to begin planting the seeds of positivity and success. Take advantage of these moments and you will be back in control of your mind in no time.

If, however, you find yourself in a place where your negative perennial thoughts have fully taken over your life and these efforts are still not working, sometimes you are only left with one choice: hitting the reset button. This is akin to pulling up everything in the garden—weeds, trees, grass, and the like and starting over with a fresh new plot of land. Honestly, it can really be a refreshing feeling, and it may be necessary to move forward. Everyone's reset button is different. For some, it means crying out to God and accepting his deliverance. For others, it is reaching out for professional help. It can even be leaving your abusive significant other before any more harm can be done. In all of these cases, the decision must be made to begin anew and get help. It takes you coming to the end of yourself and reaching a place where you feel completely broken in pride. At that point, you can begin the process of change.

ANDREW G. MCDONALD

    Many people are in this harrowing position and do not even know it; so if you are one of these people, do not feel bad. I myself have had to hit the reset button once or twice in my life. It is tough, but once it is done, the weight will be lifted from your shoulders. During my parents' nasty divorce, I was in dire mental straits. Walking into my house after school was the most nerve-racking experience for me. What was it going to be today? Never-ending bickering and arguing? Broken plates and glasses? Or worse, mental manipulation to serve the needs of one spouse versus another?

    I distinctly remember coming home early after school one day because band practice had been cancelled. I walked in the door to my mother screaming "Your name better be on the mortgage if you're coming in here! Do not dare take another step otherwise." Half of me wanted to heed her warning and go right back out the door. She quickly calmed down and apologized after she realized I was the one standing there, the unintended recipient of a poison-filled, hurt-inducing message, but it was these types of experiences that filled me with anxiety growing up. After a while, my mood began to plummet. My thoughts, filled with screaming, crying, and pain, made me feel miserable. It was even affecting me physically. Depression was weighing me down to the point of my shoulders physically hunching forward and my attention permanently fixed to the ground in front of me.

    It was at this point in my life that I knew, even as young as I was, that somehow I had to change. Therefore, I hit the reset button. I decided on that day that I was going to change my mood whether I liked it or not. I began standing taller, rolling back my shoulders, and sticking out my chest in the midst of turmoil. I began venting to my closest friends about my situation, no matter how agonizing or embarrassing the truth was. I began continually reminding myself that if I could only make it through this phase in my life, if I could only weather the storm, then I could make it through just about anything. I even began reaching out to God and praying more.

It worked. My mood began improving. I began to smile more. The screaming and arguing, although still painful to witness, did not quite affect me in the same way as it had before. I hit the reset button, laid the seeds of perseverance, and vigorously defended them from the weeds that tried to take hold of my psychological landscape. Not only did I emerge victorious from the battle, but I was able to use that triumph to motivate me in other trials as well.

Again, do not be afraid to ask for help in hitting the reset button. I know many people who suffer in silence because they refuse to accept that they need help in their lives. Some of it has to do with fear—the fear of embarrassment or the fear of judgment by others. A lot of it has to do with pride; they believe they do not need the help or that they can do it on their own. Diseases like depression, anxiety, and bipolarity (just to name a few) are simply too great an obstacle to overcome by one's self. Just as an actor cannot put on a Broadway play without the help of his or her supporting cast, directors, producers, and background staff, we cannot hope to stage a complete revamp of our minds without the help of those around us.

Use your mind generously and purposefully. There is a lot of power and potential stored in between your two earlobes that is just waiting to be tapped. Although sometimes you will have to fight vigorously in order to protect your goals, dreams, and even your sanity, we have been equipped with the weapons to defeat the annual and perennial weeds that sprout up. By using methods like prevention (building up knowledge and confidence levels before negative thoughts and emotions surface), weed-killers (using positive thoughts and experiences as ammunition to cancel out the negative ones), and the reset button (deciding that enough is enough and resolving to seek help from others), you will begin to see true changes and, ultimately, successes in your life.

Behold the Power of Words!

"The words you speak can affect your goals and to what level you will achieve them." **Audrey Marlene Johann**

One of the most powerful lessons my mother instilled in me was the second step in the Limitless Success Method: to "Speak It." I distinctly recall my mother sitting me in front of a mirror during times of low self-esteem and forcing me to recite the words "I AM somebody." Saying it one time was not enough. I would have to say it repeatedly until I sounded like I believed it. I found it slightly embarrassing then, but over time a funny thing happened: I actually began to believe it! It was not just a half-belief, either; it became truth, like the color of my skin or the number of toes on my feet. Steadily developing confidence in myself, I started acting as if I was somebody. I began to stand just a little bit taller. I began to speak just a little bit louder. I developed a purpose: to prove to the world just how much of a "somebody" I was. Behold the power of words! Thinking and dreaming about a particular goal or objective will never become real without actually speaking it into existence. Imagine if Thomas Edison had stopped at *thinking* about the light bulb, or if Whitney Houston had only *thought* about becoming a multi-genre phenom. Something is magical and beyond logical human explanation about speaking a word out into the universe. I can think of no better example of "Speaking It" than one man's four-word phrase that transformed him into a champion. Four. Simple. Words.

ANDREW G. MCDONALD

    This man was simply excellent at his craft. He prepared diligently and refined his physique and skills to near perfection. He was not extremely intelligent, as he willingly admits, but he did not let that hold him back. What he did not have in education, he more than made up for in skilled athleticism and tenured experience. When this man talked, people listened. He talked often, most of it nothing but smack. He had a confidence—perhaps even an arrogance—about him that drove people (namely his opponents) crazy. But to his defense, he consistently backed it up with win after win. Then, one day, before millions of viewers, he uttered the four-word phrase: "I am The Greatest."

    Of course, people either laughed off his unequaled brashness or scoffed at his narcissism—that is, until he put his doubters to shame with his victory over Sonny Liston in 1964. The nickname then stuck. Now, whenever you hear the moniker "The Greatest," most people will automatically assume the person is referring to "The Greatest" boxer of all time, Muhammad Ali. Do you know why he is the greatest boxer of all time? Because he said that he was. He spoke the words "I am The Greatest" and it became reality for both him and the world. I highly doubt that he would be near the legend that he is today without that crass mouth of his. You can argue with his overconfidence, but you cannot argue with the results!

    If you remember, in Chapter 5 we discussed how thoughts are simply seeds that, with the right amount of nurture and care, can grow and bear fruit in your life. This requires continuous watering of your seeds in your mind. What Ali was doing that others were not was just that: watering the seeds. He used his power and authority to speak positive things into the universe that did not exist for him before. When Ali said that he was the greatest, there was one problem: it was not true—yet. However, because he planted the seeds in his mind and used the "eloquence" of his poetic rhymes and lyrics to water them, he was able to harvest, eventually, the spoils of victory. And not only was he able to plant the seeds of greatness in his mind, but these seeds were sown in the minds of everyone who watched him fight (or just happened to be on the other side of his boxing gloves!).

As mentioned, there is something almost magical about speaking a thought into existence. It is like ordering room service and the universe catering to your needs and appetite on a silver platter. Once you have the thinking portion down pat, the next step is to physically speak your thoughts out loud. "Okay," you might say. "I understand why positive thinking is so important. However, I would really feel silly speaking out loud, even in the quiet of my own company. Why should we actually care so much about what we speak? What makes our words so powerful?" Well, allow me to explain this principle in both a biblical and a practical context.

In the Bible (Proverbs 18:21, to be exact), King Solomon states that "Death and life are in the power of the tongue: and they that love it shall eat the fruit thereof." What he was saying was that what you speak carries great weight. This is further exemplified in Jesus' meeting with a fig tree quite a few books later in Matthew 21 and Mark 11.

To emphasize, a judge and jury can condemn a person to death or choose to exonerate them from wrongdoing. The Federal Reserve Chairperson can cause harmony or discord throughout the entire nation based on just a few choice words in his or her speech. A person has the power to break or repair the heart of a loved one by using or omitting the words "do not" in the sentence "I love you." God gave us this power, and we should use it early, often, and judiciously.

In a practical sense, let us examine three examples for you that should further convince you of this power: Asch's line judgment experiment, hypnosis, and Loftus's misinformation study.

Asch's Line Judgment Experiment

In 1955, a psychologist by the name of Solomon Asch set out to determine how far people would go to conform to a group. Therefore, he did what any other hypothesis-wielding scientist would do: he designed an experiment. In this case, he had seven people enter a room. Each was told they were there to compare the length of some lines in a series of rounds. The administrator then held up two cards. One card contained a straight vertical line. The other card contained three other lines of various lengths. The administrator at this point asked each participant from left to right which line on the second card was similar to the line on the first. Astonishingly enough, the first six people picked the wrong line! It was not as if the lines on the second card were very similar in length as well; it was glaringly obvious that these participants had chosen poorly.

When it came time for the seventh participant to choose, they were as bewildered as any of us would have been. How could these people choose the wrong line? Are you kidding me? Well, unbeknownst to them, the other six participants were actually confederates, people specifically asked to give the wrong answer. However, what is truly astonishing about this study was that after multiple trials, when it came down to the seventh participant, a whopping 76% of them went along with the group and chose the wrong answer at least once even though they knew with full certainty that the answer was wrong. This was either because they did not want to embarrass themselves by not conforming to the crowd, or they were somehow convinced that *they* were wrong and the crowd was correct. What is more astounding is that when these same people took the test themselves, less than one percent answered incorrectly.

What can we gain from this experiment? We can conclude that not only will people conform to a majority, but also that with enough negative or incorrect statements, people will eventually succumb to that negative or incorrect belief. For instance, look at the data: 76% of the true participants conformed at least once to giving the wrong answer. In addition, 11% of these individuals gave the wrong answer along with the group every time they were asked. This likely means that 89% of them initially resisted conformity but eventually fell to it in later rounds. When looking at this from a success perspective, imagine you are the seventh participant. Instead of lines, the administrator holds up a headshot of you, and asks the other six people in the room whether they think you are a success or a failure in life based on the photo. One by one, each of the six answers "failure." Would you answer "failure" as well? How about after five rounds? Ten? What about after years and years of rounds?

Hypnosis

Furthermore, we have the ability to influence our mind and feelings on a subconscious level by "Speaking It" as well. My horrifying experience with hypnosis will surely convince you of that. A couple of years ago, my wife and I attended a local renaissance festival. She is a huge fan of all things medieval, renaissance, and fantasy, so this was the perfect venue for her to let her proverbial hair down and enjoy fellowship with those who enjoy it as much as she does. I, on the other hand, was less enthused but could dig the sights and sounds of the festival, and if anything, it was ripe for people watching. To satisfy my curiosity and support my all-in wife, I dressed up alongside her and enjoyed the ride.

On this particular trip, however, there was a show given by a traveling hypnotist. Intrigued, I asked my wife if she would like to stop by. "At the very least, it should be entertaining," I explained. Hesitantly, she obliged, and before I knew it, we were on our way to watch the show. I knew it was going to be interactive, but what happened next was nothing short of shocking. The man introduced himself and his profession and asked us to close our eyes and relax. This was not a normal mode of relaxation, he explained, and encouraged us to relax even more. "I want you to feel as if your limbs are as heavy as twenty pound weights as you drift further and further into a deeper sleep," he told us. Astonishingly enough, I consented to his request and began to feel myself more relaxed than I have ever felt! The hypnotist must have sensed this, because before long he pulled me up on stage with some other "volunteers." Oh, God, I thought nervously. I am now a part of the main feature in his act!

Everything he spoke after that moment seemed to be a good idea, so I went with it. I was asked to perform many embarrassing tasks, like pretend to ride in a space shuttle, cluck like a chicken, and even forget my own name! It was a surreal experience because I knew what I was doing and I was in full control, but whatever he said sounded logical, so I obliged. Sleeping when he said to sleep, standing when he said to stand, traveling distant lands in my imaginary spaceship all of a sudden sounded like brilliant ideas. Deep down I knew it was humiliating, but his soothing, trusting words convinced me otherwise.

POSSESS YOUR SUCCESS: MASTERING THE LIMITLESS SUCESS METHOD

When we were finally released from his "control," I walked up to my wife, who was about as embarrassed as I was. When she asked about the experience, I described it in full detail: the relaxing of my body, the absurd suggestions that all of a sudden made sense, the feeling of being in control and yet being a prisoner in my own body. "Well, I hope you got what you wanted," she said with a slight "I told you so" in her voice. Yeah, I thought. I received much more than what I bargained for, that was for sure.

At that point, I knew I had experienced firsthand the power of words. The hypnotist's words did not force me to do anything; instead, he made me want to do them. He was able to tap into my subconscious without any brute force or powerful hospital machinery. All he needed to do was speak things into my life, and my mind and body relented. You see, that is how hypnosis works. The hypnotist makes a suggestion when the subject is in a quasi-sleep state, and the subconscious (one of the most powerful parts of the brain) decides what to do with it. The subject can decide to either accept or reject the suggestion, but because of the sleep state he or she is in, the subject's normal rationale is restricted, thus making those suggestions more convincing.

This power to influence your mind and body is not limited to hypnotists. We all have the innate ability to change how we feel or what we can do with our words. It is actually very easy to do so, too. It first takes the knowledge, the faith, and the belief that what you say has the ultimate power in your life. You need to know beyond all doubt that you can speak things into existence. The second requirement is to actually begin speaking your thoughts and dreams into the universe. Many religious and spiritual individuals talk about confessing your blessings. What they mean is, when you confess something, you are telling the universe that you are going to get your blessing. The universe at that point has to respond, and either you will get what you asked for or you will not. However, by speaking positive confessions and eliminating negative ones, the universe will eventually have to give you what you want. This is how God set the universe up to be; it is up to you to follow the rules or not.

If you have ever heard of a self-fulfilling prophecy, it is the direct result of confessions either on the behalf of the individual, or by those around him that are continuously speaking things into his life. As demonstrated in Asch's line judgment experiment, this person may initially resist, disregarding the notion they say or hear from others as a joke or false statement, but with enough repetitive statements made to or by them, subconsciously the statements become believable. If they were told or told themselves that they were a smashing success, the individuals would believe they were successful, and thus become successful. If they were told or told themselves that they were a massive failure, then ultimately the individual would believe that, failing miserably and often. In each case, they would be bound to the words that were spoken into their lives, and their words have a high impact on their course in life.

Loftus's Misinformation Study

Envision yourself at the scene of a horrific car accident. You happen to be walking by, simply enjoying the fresh air, when suddenly a turning car at an intersection with a stop sign gets T-boned by another automobile heading in the opposite direction. As the tow trucks, paramedics, and police attempt to clean up the scene and make sense of things, you are asked to fill out a police report and answer a few questions about what you witnessed. The first question the police officer asks you is "How fast were the cars going when they smashed into each other over by that yield sign?" How would you respond?

Words are so incredibly powerful that they can actually affect and alter a person's memory! In fact, psychologist Elizabeth Loftus successfully proved just that in her experiments concerning car accidents. Participants in this experiment were asked to view a complex event (i.e. the car accident scenario above) and then answer questions about what they saw. At first glance, it seemed like a very straightforward task. However, for some participants, misinformation was given in the questions, such as referencing a yield sign when it was clearly a stop sign, or asking the question "How fast were the cars going when they *smashed* into each other?" versus "How fast were the cars going when they *hit* each other?"

Interestingly enough, those that had been told about a yield sign more often than not reported they remembered seeing a yield sign instead of a stop sign. Why would the participants remember vivid details about an event that were not true? Because of the power of words, of course. One word single-handedly changed the memory of another person and tricked him or her into believing something that was not real. Furthermore, we see this again when asked about cars being "smashed" instead of "hit." People who were given the word "smashed" when asked about car speeds reported faster speeds on average than those who were given the word "hit," demonstrating the effectiveness of words on an individual's memory performance.

As if this was not enough proof, Loftus decided to take it a step further. The people who received the words "smashed" and "hit" were then asked to come back a week later to answer more questions, one of which was "Did you see any broken glass?" Predictably, those who received the word "smashed" were more likely to have "witnessed" broken glass, even though there was no glass in the scene. It seems these participants made up the broken glass in order to support their false memory of two cars smashing into each other.

To further drive this point home, the words people speak into your life can have a profound effect on your psyche. It can cause you to think things that are not true and cause you to react in line with what has been said. In this same way, you are able to use these words to change your mind, your body, or even your personal circumstances. All it takes is one word into the universe and you may have what you asked for. However, if you are not careful with your words, it can end up hurting you instead of helping you. At this moment, I would like to introduce to you the concept of poisoning the water well.

A negative confession about your mood may cause you to become depressed. Complaining about your debt could lead to more debt. Telling your kids how foolish and reckless they are will likely lead to even more tomfoolery in the future. This is what happens when you poison the water well. Imagine a very small town in the old days that uses a water well to provide refreshment and hydration to all its residents. Regrettably, by some misfortune (either accidental or otherwise) the well becomes contaminated. Those who continue to drink from this poisoned well will now become sick, diseased, or worse. The only prudent thing to do at this point is to dig another well, which requires lots of hard labor and reduplicated effort. Not to mention all of the poor souls that must now go without water until the project is complete.

That is what happens when you poison the water well. Using your words, you speak poison into your life and the lives of others. Others, because of your negativity, in turn become negative themselves. What is worse is that you begin to speak negative events into the universe and they actually happen, not only in your life, but also the lives of others. It is a very contagious problem with difficult solutions. If you are the poisoned water well, you must make every effort to clean up your act. As in the case of the weeds in the garden, prevention is the best solution, but if that is not possible because it has already happened, it is time to turn to using positive words. When someone speaks negativity into your life, instead show him or her kindness. If you fall into misfortune, such as a higher-than-expected bill or a bad car accident, you must "Speak It" as though you have the money to pay and the healing to get through such a troubling time. It will take much discipline, effort, and patience, but will pay off handsomely when implemented consistently.

If, on the other hand, someone else is the poisoned water well, then you have an equally difficult decision to make. You can either avoid them like the plague or work with them to help clean up their detrimental mindset and speech habits. Avoiding a toxic influence is easy when it is someone that is not close to you, such as a co-worker or a friend-of-a-friend. However, if it is your boss, or your mother, or your spouse, is it so easy to just walk away from them? What should you do? In this instance, you may have little choice but to help them to do better.

Instead of seeing it as a chore or burden, change your perspective and view it as an opportunity. Helping others to become more positive has multiple benefits. It not only helps the person become more successful in their endeavors, but it also instills the principles of positive thinking and speaking that are involved in the Limitless Success Method, bolstering your confidence and knowledge in the subject matter. Finally, and perhaps even more importantly, you might possibly have spared those that will come in contact and interact with that person the negativity and pessimism that will likely spew out of them.

Essentially, our success may be short-circuited by the words we speak. It is incredible and yet so true. The best thing that you can do to remedy consistent failures is to monitor, control, and enhance your vocabulary with positivity and optimism. When we choose to have a dim outlook on our path to success, we end up talking ourselves out of valuable opportunities to grow and develop because we either fear loss or simply believe we do not deserve it. When we say that we expect bad things to happen, they often do because we attract that which we speak. We need to be much more judicious with our words, because as the saying goes: "Be careful what you wish for; you just might get it."

Putting Words into Action

One of the biggest obstacles that kept me from verbally voicing positive thoughts, feelings, and emotions was the fear of embarrassment and/or humiliation. Honestly, I used to feel downright dumb doing it. "Who in the world talks to themselves?" I would think self-consciously. Even in times of complete seclusion with no one around to hear or judge me, I would still have trouble. It really took a lot of prayer and practice to finally feel comfortable speaking things I wanted to happen out loud. During the struggle, I had to come to terms with the fact that it was my self-consciousness and pride that was holding me back. My self-consciousness would tell me I was silly for taking that step, while my pride would tell me I did not even need to take that step in the first place.

After this grand epiphany, I knew what I needed to do: quash my self-consciousness and swallow my pride. However, at first it was a bit difficult. I had to develop a confidence about myself that honestly just was not there. Similar to working out or learning a new trade, exercising your faith for the first time is awkward, and I was not very good at it. Nevertheless, as I remained consistent and began witnessing the power of my words, I started speaking with a boldness and authority I never knew existed. Within a week, I had thoroughly convinced myself that my words had immeasurable amounts of influence and what I was saying would, in fact, happen.

Another surefire suggestion I would like to provide you with combines "Speaking It" with the potent visualization technique outlined in Chapter 2. To execute correctly, place visuals of what you desire in your life around the house or workplace. It does not always have to be a picture. In fact, for even greater effect, use a written statement of your ability to accomplish, find, or purchase that desired item instead. Surprisingly enough, people have been doing it for years and it is truly a motivating force if used appropriately. I am sure you have seen desktop backgrounds of white, sandy beaches or sexy, powerful convertibles. You may even see statements of faith or inspiration around someone's home or office cubicle. However, where people go wrong is by stopping at the visual. While simply placing these visuals where you can see them is effective in the short run, after a while these extravagant images become decorations while simply fading into the background, just like the many dreams of achieving or owning those items.

So what is a person to do to keep focused on these visuals? The answer is very simple. Every time you see or pass by the visual, recite a statement of future ownership or continual empowerment. What I mean is, if the visual is textual, such as a quote saying "Faith. Family. Friends." and this is in line with your values or what you desire your family's values to be, then every time you pass by that quote on the wall or by your desk, simply state it out loud or make a positive confession, such as "My family values faith, family, and friends, and with these we are content." If your goal or dream is to tour across the livable six continents of the world, then post pictures of the destinations. Every time those images catch your eye, state "I will find a way to visit each of these destinations," followed by the actual list of destinations. Be specific but brief, because the last thing you want to do is spend five to ten minutes per visit reciting confessions.

As strong as this tactic is, I realize we live in the real world. Sometimes we forget to make our confession, and a recital on every passing may be a bit much for us. That is okay. The goal is not to make it a tedious chore. Remember that without confidence and faith in what you are saying, your confessions become meaningless words and can further delay your goals and dreams. The key is being consistent. If you feel you need to make your verbal confession every time you pass by your visual reminder, then go for it. If once a day works for you, this is fine as well. Just be sure that you are continually applying step one and step two of the Limitless Success

Method to these goals and dreams and you will begin to discover opportunities for progress in attaining them.

One of the habits I have developed that has directly contributed to my confidence and overall success was a spiritual confession given to me by my pastor. One day, as I was walking into the service, the ushers were passing around small index-card-sized advertisements, similar to the promotions you might find on your car window. One side of the card was an ad highlighting a book my pastor had recently written. The other side, however, was where I found my true value. On that side were the words:

> I declare that **I WIN** over every battle all the time, and my God always causes me to triumph. No test or trial of my faith will cause me to give up, cave in, or quit. Failure is not final, and I will not stop until **I WIN**. I am more than a conqueror in Christ Jesus. My victory is guaranteed because God loves me, and the shed blood of Jesus gives me a right to win in every area of my life. **I WIN** in my marriage. **I WIN** in my finances. **I WIN** in my job. **I WIN** over unemployment. **I WIN** over negative emotions. I WIN over selfishness. **I WIN** in my physical body. **I WIN** over lack. I refuse to be contained by the enemy or my flesh ever again! I am breaking out and I am breaking through today because **I WIN! I WIN! I WIN!** I declare these words this day and it is so, in the name of Jesus. Amen!

At the time, this revelation was huge for me. I had just moved to the city of Atlanta, away from all of my friends and family (the only person I knew outside of work was my wife). Due to moving costs and health issues, money was becoming extremely tight. Anxiety was at an all-time high and I began to spiral into depression. Although I shortly found a church I liked, I felt lost and confused, and

I ached for some sort of positive change. It really felt as if my drive and joy were near dead.

However, this bold, fresh confession breathed new life into me! It provided the faith and confidence in my Creator that I had lost sight of and desperately needed to regain. I quickly took it home and placed it in the bottom corner of my bathroom mirror. This way, as I reached for my toothbrush in the morning, I would be reminded of the control God gave to me over my life. Every day I would recite it meticulously until it was fully etched into my permanent memory. That was when things began to change. As my confidence and faith grew, I began developing friendships and feeling much more energetic. I would wake in the morning fired up and ready to tackle the day's obstacles. Even the most difficult days were made easier by simply rehearsing that one confession. To this day, that confession card still sits in the bottom corner of my bathroom mirror, a constant reminder of the authority exercised on my life because I put those potent words into action.

Now that you grasp the concept of speaking things into existence, it is important to understand a hidden danger of speaking confessions aloud. Picture this: You are currently in the middle of your college career, having a great time and ignoring your slowly slipping grades. After you receive your less-than-stellar grades back at the end of the semester, you suddenly have a grand epiphany: Shoot! If I do not turn things around quick, I could really ruin my future! Thus, you set the challenging goal to study 10 hours per week to get your grades up. What do you do next? Many will go out and tell their friends and family about their noble and virtuous goal. After all, you want to be held accountable. In addition, it feels so good when others throw their support behind you and congratulate you on your ambitions.

POSSESS YOUR SUCCESS: MASTERING THE LIMITLESS SUCESS METHOD

Unfortunately, you may also be sabotaging your own success if you go that route. That is correct: the more you talk about your goals and dreams to others, the less likely you will actually follow through on your intentions. It has nothing to do with the haters and dream-killers, either. In fact, your loyal supporters would actually be the culprits working against you in this regard (can somebody say, "Et tu, Brute?"). Most of us have it in our minds that it is a good thing to tell those close to us about our purposeful plans. However, the mind is a very mysterious place, and sometimes even the best of intentions can have the opposite effect on a person's psyche.

The explanation behind such a controversial statement is due to what is called "social reality," the mind's way of forming a perceived reality based on the awareness of others. There is a sense of accomplishment that comes with telling others about your goals, almost as though you have already accomplished them. In essence, your mind says, "Well, that's good enough for me!" and you do not even bother with actually completing what you desire to do. In an experiment performed by Peter Gollwitzer et al, they designed four studies meant to test whether people's awareness of their subjects' intentions had an effect on an individual's ability to complete a given task. The studies not only revealed that was there a negative impact on completion rates, but they were able to prove that those who told others about their plans had already benefitted from a premature sense of accomplishment, causing them to lag far behind the progress of those who did not tell anyone about their plans.

Keep in mind, however, that this is not contradictory to speaking words into existence as discussed previously in this chapter. Formerly, it was explained that words have power and that speaking those words out loud will have a tremendous effect on whether you will achieve your wants and desires in life. Unfortunately, speaking these words to others can open you up to all kinds of unintended consequences. You must strike a balance between speaking too little and speaking too much.

Now, you may be asking yourself how you could possibly avoid this pitfall while still keeping yourself accountable to realize your goals and dreams. The first thing you can do is be very selective about the people to whom you tell your goals and dreams. We all know the person who always clamors on to everyone about what they are doing and yet never really does anything. Now we know why they do that; they get to enjoy the satisfaction of completion without the effort! Avoid being that person; remember that, just as you must choose your words wisely, you must also choose wisely to whom you speak those words.

The second thing you can do is ensure that you only tell those who will hold you accountable to your goals and dreams, such as a coach, mentor, or trusted friend. Not only are they less likely to kill your dreams (accidentally or otherwise), but they are also less likely to congratulate you for nothing. These individuals should know you very well and be able to see through veiled attempts to increase your ego. They also have to be able to hound you continuously until you take action.

Finally, if you do decide to express your intentions, phrase them in a way that elicits words of responsibility versus celebration. Instead of simply saying, "I'm going to study 10 hours a week," you might try saying, "do not congratulate me now, but I am going to study 10 hours a week. Do not let me quit on this, okay?" The key here is to downplay your sense of accomplishment until after you have actually done something. Otherwise, the social reality effect will kick in, reducing your motivation to make good progress towards your goals.

You will need to take all of these steps in order for your words to have power. You are required to humble yourself enough to accept that positive words are necessary and develop the courage to speak them. It will also take a consistent effort for "Speaking It" to work, so make it a persistent habit in your life, replacing the old habit of speaking negative and cynical words. However, once you have this step down, you will be surprised at the results. Money will begin to come into your life. Healing will find its way into your body. Happiness will return to you. Your career will begin to blossom. Most of all, opportunities for success and prosperity will follow you wherever you go.

The 5 Essential Forces of Success

By reading the first several chapters of this book you should have developed the ability to think and speak positively with purpose, increasing your chances for success tenfold. A congratulation is in order; a good 80-90% of your success will come from consistently applying the principles of "Thinking It" and "Speaking It." You have begun to renew your mind and clear out those annoying "weeds"—any negative thought or emotion that deters you from your goal.

You should also be trained to speak life into yourself and others. Your confessions should now be full of faith and the belief that what you said will ultimately happen. You should be fully prepared to achieve your goals and dreams; in essence, you are ready for the final step in the Limitless Success Method: to "Do It." In this step, you will put your money where your mouth is and make your dreams a reality; you will finally set in motion the course of events that will ensure total victory.

What if I told you there were a few chosen forces that, when used collectively and consistently, would result in success in your life paralleled by no one? What if I told you that to implement what you meditated on and spoke into the universe, you would only need to use five forces? What if I told you that great people like Bill Gates, Jackie Robinson and many others have all used these forces to get where they are today? Would you believe me?

POSSESS YOUR SUCCESS: MASTERING THE LIMITLESS SUCESS METHOD

There are, in fact, five forces that, once you master, will make success almost inevitable. This upcoming chapter will aid you in developing the framework of a tried and true success strategy. You can apply these forces towards any type of goal and your strategy will be effective almost every time. These are real forces that the wealthy and successful have been using for centuries to sustain their power, prestige, and prosperity, and today I am about to teach them to you.

These forces are so powerful that they are above all other forces that will bring you success. I have studied many successful individuals, from wealthy entrepreneurs to CEO's to musicians, all the way to doctors and superstar athletes. They all have used these success forces to jumpstart their life and their career. I call these forces *The 5 Essential Forces of Success*. Each one is extremely potent on its own, but it is when they are used in addition to one another that they are most effective.

With these 5 Essential Forces, opportunities will seemingly fall out of the sky and into your lap. Success will come naturally to you, and wealth will begin to chase you instead of the other way around. You may even become more attractive because of the aura surrounding you and the positive vibes you put out. I promise, if you begin to focus on these 5 Essential Forces of Success, you will begin to see far-reaching changes in your life that will lead you to wherever you want to go.

I remember when I first uncovered these Essential Forces. At the time, I was still growing and learning, and I had this hunger for all of the things that come along with a success-filled life. I had such a deep desire to determine exactly how people continually capitalized on their success that I found myself lying awake at night just pondering over it. As I discovered more and more about these leaders, phenomes, virtuosos, and prodigies in their respective fields, I also discovered the parallels and commonalities between them. They all had these 5 simple characteristics that they were able to master and employ at will. Without these 5 forces, I truly believe they would not have come close to where they are today.

At this moment, I will reveal to you the 5 Essential Forces of Success. I will discuss what they are and provide practical applications for their use. Utilize them frequently and judiciously to implement your dreams and your visions. They are:

Drive
Ambition
Preparation
Accountability
Faith

Essential Force 1: Drive

"You can do anything as long as you have the drive." Sabrina Bryan

Definition: an inner urge that stimulates activity or inhibition; a basic or instinctive need.

Do you know what drives you? What pushes you forward every day? What gets you up each morning when you would otherwise lie in bed? Your drive is that source inside of you that moves you before you even know you have been moved, that feeling that urges you to take action in your life despite the challenges. Like the V8 engine in a Chevrolet Camaro, possessing a large amount of drive can increase your acceleration towards success almost effortlessly.

If you remember the description of the Limited as profiled in Chapter 5, as soon as they encounter the slightest resistance to their goals, these individuals will promptly throw up their hands and say "I cannot do this," a testament to their lack of drive and ability to problem-solve. On the other hand, instead of a declaration of defeat, the Limitless will pose a question: "How can I accomplish this?" This makes all the difference. You see, the drive of the Limitless will not let them give in to obstacles. They actually enjoy a sense of challenge and embrace resistance because they realize that with challenge comes creativity, and with creativity, success.

Of course, there is the question of the source of this drive that you see in the Limitless. Drive has two basic components: Motivation—the internal energy needed to progress or act in a certain way, and Passion—the emotional connection to a task, dream, or a particular subject matter.

Let us first examine how these two components work in tandem. To understand the concept better, we will revisit the example of exercise. If you think of drive as a muscle, motivation would be the carbs, the energy you will need to begin and sustain your physical activity. Meanwhile, passion would act as the protein that builds the muscle up and makes it stronger and more capable to handle the task at hand. Continuously feeding yourself with motivation and passion will not only make you more excited about your goal or dream, but it will keep your drive up when times get rough.

ANDREW G. MCDONALD

It is also important to understand the sources of these components to your overall drive. Motivation is really an external source. Those outside influences are the catalyst for which motivation is transferred to you. For instance, I have recently discovered some amazing personal empowerment and improvement podcasts, and they have quickly become some of my main sources of motivation. When someone shares their story on how they beat the odds to become a runaway success, or when someone shares a novel and creative perspective on a particular area I am passionate about, that motivation invigorates me with the desire to do something about it.

However, your drive is not always going to lead you down the right path. Just as if you were to recklessly hold your foot down on the gas in your brand new Camaro and leave your hands off the steering wheel, an unrestrained drive will likely cause you to crash and burn in your quest for success. To better illustrate this, I will provide two examples of those who have used their drive either to their advantage or detriment and the end result.

There was once a man who fought valiantly for liberty and equality towards his fellow man. He was deeply motivated by the plight of his fellow brothers and sisters impoverished and oppressed by rulers of another country. However, his spiritual beliefs called for nonviolence and love. Therefore, instead of bowing down and accepting his circumstances, his drive to see his people liberated led to hunger strikes, peaceful protests, and ultimately, the liberation of India from British rule. His name was Mohandas Karamchand Gandhi, and his drive inspired civil rights movements across the world.

POSSESS YOUR SUCCESS: MASTERING THE LIMITLESS SUCESS METHOD

There was another man who had such a drive as Gandhi. He was highly motivated by the effects of a lost war on his country, enough to desire to lead his people to grandeur and unprecedented prosperity for lifetimes to come. He was so driven towards the goal that he was willing to kill 10 million people, 6 million of whom were Jews, the people he loathed and blamed for the pitiful state of the country. His name was Adolf Hitler, and his drive led to a Second World War and the tragic deaths of millions of those who stood in his way.

These examples highlight the extremes in which your drive may lead you. A powerful force, it can truly make things happen in your life. In fact, people would starve to death if not for the drive to live and eat. However, drive is also dangerous in the wrong hands. Looking back on our earlier car example, you control both the gas pedal and the steering wheel of that Camaro. You must use both parts wisely and judiciously to have an exhilarating, but safe, ride. Without the appropriate direction and control, a hot rod can become a dangerous machine, leaving nothing behind but destruction in its wake. Likewise, using your drive recklessly can have disastrous implications in your life. Your direction and control will determine where your drive takes you.

Action Summary:
1. Never use the words "I cannot." Instead, think creatively and ask, "How can I?"
2. Fuel your drive to move forward with motivation and passion. Find your emotional connection, and use outside influences to continually inspire you to reach further.
3. Maintain control over your drive. Otherwise, it could lead to costly mistakes, unnecessary failures, and in extreme cases, destruction to yourself and those around you.

Essential Force 2: Ambition

"Ambition is a dream with a V8 engine." Elvis Presley

<u>Definition:</u> an earnest desire for some type of achievement or distinction, as power, honor, fame, or wealth, and the willingness to strive for its attainment.

Ambition is really what separates the "Talkers" from the "Doers." The Limited will talk all day about how much they can or plan to do in life, knowing very well that they will never do half of it. Why? Because their Limited views of themselves will not allow them to finish what they start, if they even begin at all.

The Limitless, on the other hand, have a firm knowledge that they can accomplish beyond what they know they can do. This affords them the freedom to proclaim, "I WILL do this!" They know that somewhere deep inside of them is the ability to achieve the unachievable, no matter how challenging or arduous the task. This, my friend, is the essence of ambition. They not only desire success but they will transform it into reality.

Accordingly, ambition is the realization that you can take a dream further, to turn it into stated, achievable goals. Each day comes with a plethora of dreams, but not every dream is meant to become a reality. Furthermore, not every dream that is meant to come to fruition actually makes it, either. It is your responsibility to take that dream or vision from its initial inception and turn it into a tangible reality.

In order to do so, I can't stress enough the importance of following the first two steps of success: "Thinking It" and "Speaking It". Once you think you can do something and announce your intentions to the universe, this will begin to build up the ambition necessary to take the next step towards "Doing It".

Generally, the ambitious mindset comes from one of two fundamental states of mind: one of confidence, or one of desperation. For example, imagine you are a programmer for a software development firm. You have been involved in this area for quite a while, and along the way, you have gained valuable experience and wisdom. What was once extremely difficult is now automatic, and your refined, well-practiced, and skilled code writing has earned you very prestigious accolades from your firm. Now you seek bigger challenges, ones your employer simply cannot provide. Thus, you decide to open up your own independent game development studio, something you have always wanted to do.

The reason for the ambition to step out on your own in spite of the fact that a large number of all startups fail, is not your good looks or your ability to charm others into requesting your products and services. No, it was because of the confidence that came from years of software development. After spending so much time practicing and fine-tuning your craft, your confidence grew to the point where you knew you were going to be successful even before you began.

On the other hand, there is another way to spur ambition. Ambition also comes out of a place of desperation. Let us say that instead of wanting to leave your current job, you are forced out due to layoffs. Many software development companies have underwent hiring freezes, making it extremely difficult to find a new job in this role. What are you to do then? You have two kids at home who need to eat.

This, perhaps surprisingly, is where ambition comes in. You essentially have no choice but to succeed in order to provide for your family, and you obviously have the skills necessary to create inventive games, so it may be a no-brainer to go into business for yourself. You may not have necessarily had the confidence in yourself, but just like a baby bird being pushed out of its nest when learning how to fly, failure is not an option. Life may force our hands more than we would like, but it may be for the better as it may also force us to display an enormous amount of courage and ambition, enough to get us onto the path to success.

Once we have an ambitious mindset established, you must essentially set a goal for yourself. The key here is that you cannot simply set any goal; your goal must be both challenging and S.M.A.R.T. (**S**pecific, **M**easurable, **A**ttainable, **R**ealistic, **T**ime-Limited). Failure to follow this S.M.A.R.T. acronym could mean that your goal will not be focused enough for you to complete. If there is no structure or challenge to complete the goal you set for yourself, you will not feel much of a sense of accomplishment, and it can actually become a hindrance to future goals.

POSSESS YOUR SUCCESS: MASTERING THE LIMITLESS SUCESS METHOD

To provide you with an example of a S.M.A.R.T. goal, let us assume you have a dream of working in the medical field. It is something you always saw yourself doing, even as a young child, and now you are a high school senior who wants to make it happen. It is not enough just to say, "I want to be in the medical field." That is too vague of a goal. It opens you up to anything from becoming a medical receptionist to becoming a pharmaceutical CEO. With so many choices, one of two things is likely to happen: you will get distracted and end up in some other profession or end up stuck in a medical profession you do not like.

What you really need to state is something like "I want to be a Nurse Practitioner by the time I am 26." Given that this position requires between 5-8 years of education, various licenses and certifications, and real-life experience, the timeframe is definitely challenging. It is also:

Specific: A particular career was chosen.

Measurable: You can measure your success by donning the title of

Nurse Practitioner.

Attainable: While challenging, with the right combination of desire, education, and focus, the goal can be reached.

Realistic: It is realistic thinking that you would actually put in the effort to become a Nurse Practitioner.

Time-Specific: There is an end date in mind (age 26).

Setting goals like this is vital to affirming your ambition. It also focuses your attention so you refrain from pursuing aimless, fruitless whims. No one enjoys wasting time or effort, so add S.M.A.R.T. goals to your success toolbox as soon as you can and you will find that your ambition (and your overall chances of success) will grow exponentially.

Action Summary:
1. To increase and best utilize ambition, set goals that are challenging enough to push you to perform at your highest level.
2. Ensure the goals that you set are S.M.A.R.T. (Specific, Measurable, Attainable, Realistic, Time-Limited) to increase your chances of accomplishing them.

Essential Force 3: Preparation

"Before anything else, preparation is the key to [sustainable] success." Alexander Graham Bell

Definition: a proceeding, measure, or provision by which one prepares for something; preparations for a journey.

Everyone seemingly desires to achieve some level of success in their life, whether that success constitutes fame, fortune, happiness, or simply a "job well done" from his or her loved ones. However, not everyone is prepared for the level of attainment that they so desire to have. Some miss opportunities for success or fail in their quest simply because they are not prepared for them. Others attain success so quickly that they cannot adjust, causing problems in their personal life that lead to failure.

You see this repeatedly with child actors and celebrities like Lindsay Lohan, Justin Bieber, and Chris Brown. They achieve a meteoric rise in fame and money as they begin their careers, and unfortunately, they lack the necessary financial, emotional, and career guidance to continue such an unsustainable trajectory. Their upbringing, social pressures, and poor advice from those around them constantly push them towards the brink of failure, although they do not quite realize how close to the edge they truly are.

With such an abundance of money and influence, they begin to feel invincible, making poor choices without the fear of recourse. While many times we see celebrities, athletes, and entertainers escape the full punishment of the law and merely get what amounts to be a slap on the wrist, if their behavior is left unchecked, it could ultimately lead to the ruin of their careers, the alienation of their family, closest friends and allies, and the destruction of their lives.

You see, what happens is, they have the ambition to take risks when the opportunities are available. However, many icons do not realize that the following formula applies to them as much as everyone else:

Ambition – Preparation = Recklessness

Therefore, when they reach celebrity status, they are unprepared and thus perform reckless acts of ineptitude and ignorance. We are all subject to the same fate if we do not prepare for the success we plan to achieve.

In order to properly plan for sustained success, you must first develop a sound success strategy. Not doing so is essentially taking a road trip without a map. Imagine driving for hours and hours with no sense of direction. You stop to take stock of your location, and you realize you have no idea where you are. You look around and see absolutely zero road signs to provide clues as to where you are going. Think of it—where are you going? How can you expect to get somewhere when you have no idea where that "somewhere" is? You are literally on the road to nowhere!

Yet that is how many people, aristocrats and common folk alike, live their lives. They do not prepare for their success and certainly do not prepare for possible failure, and when they find themselves in the inevitable crisis, they mismanage the situation to the point where it could ruin their lives. Fortunately for the rich and powerful, they have an army of lawyers, financiers, and PR consultants behind them to bail them out of bad situations. The commoners are afforded no such luxuries.

However, those who prepare for and manage their success over time can reduce much of the volatility in their lives. Take Ellen DeGeneres, for instance. Her life has not been without controversy; she not only came from waiting tables and selling vacuum cleaners to being one of comedy's most recognizable female celebrities, but also famously came out as gay on-set during her hit TV sitcom Ellen and is a staunch supporter of LGBT and animal rights. She, through hard work and smart choices, has become a household name, and yet has not once strayed from who she is. She has been able to handle the fame very well, and her humility is unmatched. However, her kindness is what really shines; she is never afraid to help those who need and/or deserve it.

POSSESS YOUR SUCCESS: MASTERING THE LIMITLESS SUCESS METHOD

Her decision to come out as gay on her TV show could have ruined her career, if not her life. Although it is much more mainstream today, homosexuality on television was very much taboo in those days. According to Biography.com's piece on the comedian, "An ABC affiliate in Birmingham, Alabama, refused to air the landmark episode. Fearing controversy, some of the show's sponsors, Daimler Chrysler among them, withdrew advertisements." The show was even cancelled just one year later. However, she was already prepared and primed for other opportunities. She had multiple acting gigs already lined up for her, hosted an award-winning comedy special, and in 2003, launched what has since become one of the most wildly popular and successful Daytime TV talk shows since Oprah. Not only was Ellen ambitious enough to take huge risks, but she was prepared to act on them in a way that paid off handsomely.

Preparation for success also means seeking out training or educational opportunities you may need to give yourself an edge over your competition and help you navigate past your obstacles. It is important to realize that you must hone your craft, skills, and/or abilities to increase your chances of success. This does not necessarily mean the formal or traditional methods of education and training, either. While degrees and certifications are great to have, and sometimes even a necessary requirement to enter into some professions, we must also look at other, less obvious forms of training as well, to supplement any gaps left by formal education.

I distinctly remember the day that this principle really made sense to me. One of my main ambitions in life is to be a successful and profitable stock market investor. The sheer potential of the stock market has enamored me ever since I was young, and I dreamed of the day when I would be paying off my liabilities with my assets as discussed in Robert Kiyosaki's self-help masterpiece,

ANDREW G. MCDONALD

Rich Dad, Poor Dad. Even more so, I yearned for the explosive financial growth that I would achieve for the relatively miniscule effort I would need to put in. It sure beats slaving away at a job for a fraction of the earnings potential, I often thought.

As a young adult with very few financial responsibilities and a very big dream, I knew that I would have to study the subject and take action. Fortunately, I was already enrolled in my MBA program. Surely, I would learn something about how to invest in the stock market! Large corporations and financial institutions are the biggest investors, so I was positive I would find business courses tailored towards such an exciting field of study. Sadly, the only course available to me was corporate finance, a nightmare tale of present value analyses, financial structuring, and correlation calculations. While I crawled out of the class with a B- and a meager understanding of dividends, market risk, and bond pricing, I had absolutely no clue how to apply any of it to personal investing.

It was not until I began asking Google for help on the matter that I found my answer. During a search one day, I happened upon an investment-training course that, for under the cost of a new Xbox, I learned how to invest confidently and successfully. I was flabbergasted at best, and somewhat miffed at worst. I spent tens of thousands of dollars on an MBA degree and barely learned anything about investing. I spent $320 on a seemingly random investing course and I had all the foundation I needed to become a successful investor. It was then that I recognized that formal education could only prepare you for so much, and the right type of training might be the one you least expect.

POSSESS YOUR SUCCESS: MASTERING THE LIMITLESS SUCESS METHOD

Of course, too much planning or training can put you in jeopardy of failure as well. There is such a thing as over-preparation, and it can be just as perilous as under preparing. Over-preparing can lead to what is known as "Analysis Paralysis," which can destroy your ambition, increase your anxiety, and stop your momentum dead in its tracks. What happens is you get so involved in the details and intricacies of your battle plan for success that you wind up never taking any action. In addition, it is all too easy to become overwhelmed by looking too far ahead.

To avoid this dreaded Analysis Paralysis, be sure to keep in mind that even the best-laid plans will regularly have flaws. There is just no conceivable way to account for all of the variables life throws at you. This is why incorporating flexibility into your plan is so vital; knowing that something will likely go wrong allows for you to keep your eyes open for that proverbial "monkey wrench." Repeatedly you will have to tweak, adjust, and sometimes even totally rework your plan in order to stay on-track with your goals and dreams of success.

As an example, let us look back to when I first graduated college. I had worked my tail off, especially during the latter two years, and it showed. I had brought my GPA up 16 percentage points, entered an internship program that provided me with invaluable business skills and real work experience, and positioned myself to graduate with four job offers on the table, one of which was with the company of my dreams, a major aerospace and defense contractor.

I desperately desired to work for this firm. The prestige of working for a leader in the field, the excitement of taking on challenging and bleeding-edge technologies, the allure of working on top-secret projects that required several layers of security clearances—all made it seem like the greatest job ever. Therefore, when I received

ANDREW G. MCDONALD

the offer letter to work at the company making over $60,000 per year, I nearly lost it. My dreams were finally coming true!

Sadly, that dream never panned out. Imagine my surprise when one day, about two weeks before I was to pack up my belongings and set out to Virginia, I woke up to the shock of my life: an e-mail titled "Offer Update". The first sentence of the e-mail read:
Dear Andrew,

> We regret to inform you that your offer for our company has been rescinded.

I had to read the line again. The offer that I had been fantasizing about for years had been suddenly withdrawn! Why? Paperwork issues resulting in a lengthy and costly delay in my background check, they cited. I sat there for a long time in earnest disbelief. My dream had been crushed due to technicalities!

However, as big a blow as this was, I knew deep inside that I was well equipped to handle it. I snapped out of it within a couple of hours and started making phone calls and writing e-mails to my internship director, my university, and other companies, looking for any employer that would have me. You see, my life's trajectory had changed in an instant; it was my job to adjust accordingly. I had a plan that forecasted me at the top of a global defense firm. I had a plan that forecasted me debt free in two years based on the salary I would be making. I had a plan that forecasted me in the Atlanta office so I could be closer to the woman that would eventually become my wife. I had to re-evaluate and rework nearly all of this (fortunately, that woman still became my wife!). As stated before, friction and obstacles will try to slow you down in life; you just need to use that friction to modify your course and keep moving forward past those obstacles.

POSSESS YOUR SUCCESS: MASTERING THE LIMITLESS SUCESS METHOD

Finally, after weeks of interviewing (and a bit of groveling I might add), I was able to nail down a job that better utilized my skillset and helped me survive, and even thrive, in the midst of a global recession (Not too shabby of a Plan B if you ask me!). However, it was all about the pivot point. Such a deflating event could have really grounded an individual that had such high hopes and aspirations in life. Preparation can only do so much, and when a curveball is headed your way, you must understand how to be flexible enough to change direction. To quote Herbert Kaufman, "The habit of persistence is the habit of victory."

I cannot emphasize enough how crucial proper preparation is to your success. Prosperous entrepreneurs, doctors, investors, builders, and anyone else who intends to do anything meaningful detail the steps to achieve their goals. They also understand the importance of flexibility and not looking too far ahead with their intentions. It is okay not to have everything figured out when you embark on an ambitious quest that coaxes you out of your comfort zone. It is silly, however, to have nothing planned. Even if you make it by chance, it will be extremely difficult to maintain a high level of success flying by the seat of your pants. Without the proper preparation, you are much more likely to crash and burn than cross the finish line.

Action Summary:
1. When you set out to achieve a goal, preparation is crucial. Create a plan and an overall strategy to help uncover some of the "hows" on your journey.
2. Look for education and training opportunities, even in the least

formal or likely of places.

3. Incorporate flexibility into your plan. Understand that you will never anticipate every situation, so adjustments along the way will be necessary.

4. Avoid "Analysis Paralysis," the result of over-planning and thus becoming overwhelmed, by a) keeping sight of the main goal and b) understanding that achieving success is an art, not a science. Sometimes, thinking only a couple of steps ahead is the best way to make progress.

Essential Force 4: Accountability

"Accountability breeds response-ability" Stephen Covey

<u>Definition</u>: the state of being accountable, liable, or answerable.

Have you ever dealt with a person who talks but never executes? How frustrating it is when they discuss all of their grandiose schemes and dreams, but when it is time to put their money where their mouth is, they are nowhere to be found!

On the other hand, how about a person who blames others for their own shortcomings? This could be your sibling, your friend, or even your boss. No matter how painfully obvious it is that they are the issue, they always find some creative way to pin their current circumstances on others!

It is easy to diagnose these mentalities as an absence of focus or problems with facing reality. However, when you really get down to it, these two types of people have a deficiency in accountability. Accountability is taking responsibility for your actions or your lack thereof. Without a sense of accountability, your intentions will always be thwarted by the newest idea that pops into your head, and those closest to you will begin to grow tired of the constant finger pointing. Worse, a lack of accountability leads to a lack of integrity, causing you to alienate further those around you through lies and deceit.

I learned the tough lessons of accountability early on as a child. I specifically recall one experience that virtually cured me of ever having to worry about such an issue. When I was young, my family and I would take annual vacations to an outdoor camping resort in the beautiful Pocono Mountains of Pennsylvania. The nature trails and indoor and outdoor water parks were a blast, but my favorite attraction—the arcade (as silly as that may sound, being on camping grounds and all)—was what made the trip worth waiting all year for! This haven for video-gaming aficionados had all of my favorite games, and many an hour would be spent saving the world from various intergalactic and mutant threats.

However, weeks before one particular trip, I had gotten myself grounded for continually acting up in class. My parents did allow me to go on the trip (likely because they could not find anyone to babysit), but I was forbidden from any fun activities. This meant no television, no water park, and, to my disappointment, no video games! What was I supposed to do with all of that time? I mean, what is the point of going camping if you could not play any video games, right?

In any case, I found a quasi-workaround. I was not allowed to play any video games, but I was still technically allowed to visit the arcade. Therefore, I would spend my hours of punishment watching others, almost playing vicariously through them. It was not the same, but it was the next best thing.

ANDREW G. MCDONALD

One day while I was patrolling the arcade, looking for people to watch, I happened upon some kids playing pool. I began to walk away to another part of the arcade when I saw them: a large stack of quarters on the side of the pool table in all of its glory. I swear those quarters were sparkling and shining brighter than any quarters I have ever seen. I am sure those people would not miss two of them, I reasoned. Thus, I waited until they seemed distracted with their game, snatched a couple quarters from the stack, and immediately made a beeline towards one of the gaming consoles. What a rush!

Not too much later, I saw my mother out of the corner of my eye walking towards me with one of the kids I lifted the quarters from! She did NOT look happy. She proceeded sternly to ask me if I took the quarters from the group of children. In response, I promptly denied any such wrongdoing. She asked me again, this time with a bit more controlled fury in her voice. I could tell this was not going to end well, but as any kid in serious trouble would do, I lied through my teeth. "You have one more chance," my mother declared. The anger was seeping out of her pores but somehow she was able to keep her tone barely above her "inside" voice. "Did you take any quarters from these children?" By this time, I was balling my eyes out. Not only had I stolen from the kids, but also I was bald-faced lying about it in spite of the fact that everyone knew I did it! Yet I still managed to stammer, "No."

What happened next was a whirlwind. Despite the walk back to the campsite being the longest, most depressing walk I have ever taken, we got back to the trailer all too soon. I promptly began receiving the worst spanking of my entire life! It was not so much because of the intensity, but because of the dread; I was to receive another spanking before we left for home, and yet another when we made it back! One spanking for each lie, she had explained. Suffice it to say, I learned a great deal about accountability that day: if you are big enough to take an action, you should be big enough to accept the consequences of that action. Not only that, but to learn and grow from those consequences, you must take responsibility. Years later, I still found myself blaming those kids for snitching on me and ruining my trip, but after some time I realized that I would have never been in that position if it were not for my bad behavior before the trip even began.

I am sure most people know at least one complainer at work. They are the one who sits there every day and moans about their unfulfilling job. I had such a co-worker when I started my first job out of college, and I even allowed their constant groaning to affect my view of my situation; after all, misery loves company, right?

It was like a page straight out of the book *Who Moved My Cheese?* By Spencer Johnson: two mice, waiting for our organization to provide us with the cheese we needed to survive in life. He started a year before me in the same mind-numbing entry-level position with inadequate pay. It was quite frustrating to be in a position where we knew we were worth much more and could be performing more fulfilling work. Many days were spent criticizing the menial aspects of our job with reckless abandon and imagining our perfect dream jobs after we could escape this workhouse. Over time, I grew tired of complaining. While my counterpart was perfectly content with sitting in misery, I was beginning to feel restless. Grumbling was not getting me any closer to leaving or moving up within the company, and I soon realized that I would have to take charge of the situation.

ANDREW G. MCDONALD

After this epiphany, I saw things differently. I owned up to the fact that I had chosen the position I was in, and only I could change it. At that point, I was able to take some tangible steps to get the job I wanted. I decided to share my thoughts with my co-worker and he agreed, albeit a bit surprised. We then decided to take the necessary steps to get to the next level. In order to keep ourselves accountable, we agreed we would check in with each other every few months.

I began to seek out various job openings within and without the firm to determine the skills I needed to advance. This was when I enrolled in an MBA program in order to boost my business and leadership acumen. I then began sharpening the technical skills and the business skills I acquired through my education and experience to make myself more marketable. I even began taking on more advanced work to keep myself challenged and engaged. All the while, my co-worker and I began talking less and less. He seemed more interested in being complacent than being successful, opting to make excuses for himself as to why he could not make any meaningful progress, often blaming it on the company, its "terrible" promotions, and its unfair politics. I soon realized that if I wanted to remain accountable to myself, I would have to keep interactions with those types of negative influences to a minimum.

After three long years, as I was finishing my MBA coursework, I finally hit pay dirt. I was able to land a new position making 20% more than I was at my old gig. This was a huge increase in pay in addition to a much more fulfilling role than before. The learning experience taught me the value of accountability in improving your circumstances. Only when I took ownership of my present circumstances was I able to move forward and progress. Blaming your problems on others will only make you more comfortable where you are at, causing you to continually "play the victim" and wallow in self-pity. If you want to enjoy Limitless success, you will have to become accountable for every decision and action you make.

I rarely talk to that Limited co-worker anymore. I did reach out to him a while back simply to catch up and see if he had made any progress. To that day, he was still working in that same old role, still complaining about how much he hated his job.

Remember, accountability gets things done and keeps you honest while doing it. Excuses, self-victimization, and fear all play into lacking this crucial force. Once you rid yourself of these limiting factors, you are free to learn and grow from previous mistakes. More importantly, it has ripple effects on your ambition and drive. Once you begin to hold yourself accountable to the end of an endeavor, you will be more ambitious and motivated to push your limits beyond what anyone (including yourself) believes you can do.

Action Summary:
1. Holding yourself accountable for your mistakes drives the learning process and makes it possible to achieve your success.
2. Accountability partners are a great tool to foster drive, perseverance, and responsibility. Be cautious, though, as choosing the wrong partner can often have the opposite effect!
3. "Playing the victim" will leave you complacent, lonely, and frustrated, and is reserved only for those who place limits on their abilities and their success.

Essential Force 5: Faith

"Faith is to believe what you do not see; the reward of this faith is to see what you believe." Saint Augustine

<u>Definition:</u> belief that is not based on proof.

It is easy to feel good about your decisions when things are going well, but not so much when it seems the world is crumbling all around you and success is far from ever becoming a reality in your life. This is where faith comes in. Faith is the lifesaver that keeps you afloat in the midst of the storm, just when you feel like you have been thrown overboard. It is the confidence that helps you take the next step even though you have no clue what is in front of you. It is the one thing that will keep you sustained when people try to tear you down and cast doubt into your mind. It allows you to dream big and act on those dreams without a shred of tangible proof that things will ever work out.

Some place their faith in their Creator, while others place their faith in themselves, their work, or their environment. While the debate of religion is very much out of the scope of this book, it is vital that you place your faith in *something*. A wise individual once said, "If you stand for nothing, you will fall for anything." I believe that this also applies to the notion of faith as well. If you do not place your faith in something, you will constantly live in a world of fear and paranoia, accomplishing absolutely nothing because you do not trust anything you do to work.

We constantly take for granted our faith in our environment nearly every day. It may sound silly, but the truth is we place our faith in the ground every day, believing it will not suddenly split apart and swallow us whole. When we walk out the house, we place our faith in the locks on our doors, assuming they will help prevent thieves from breaking in. We place our faith in our cars that when we drive to and from our destinations, every part will work together seamlessly and safely, from the nuts and bolts to the brakes to the engine. Moreover, as for me, I place my faith in a God who has provided me with everything I need to be consistently successful in life.

It is essential that we employ this type of faith when dealing with our goals and dreams. We must have an unshakable amount of faith even when times get tough. Fortunately, there are ways we can improve and build our faith. It all begins with diligence, the consistency of practice and repetition. Diligence brings forth the confidence to succeed, and that confidence brings forth faith. This means two things. First, that by careful study and focus on a particular area, we will become more confident in that area. Your trust in your knowledge, expertise, and skill allows you to press forward in spite of what you see or perceive. It also means we can kill multiple birds with one stone: while you are building faith, you will also be developing your ambition. Furthermore, practice is a form of preparation, and thus as you prepare it bolsters your faith.

Have you ever wondered why spiritual individuals always refer to their holy book when adversity strikes? The natural answer is because that is where their faith lies. While that is undeniably true, let us take a deeper look into *why* that is true. When a person studies a particular subject area day after day, month after month, they become well-versed in that area. As the scriptures and verses become part of their overarching philosophy, they begin to apply it into their lives. Then, when they see results, they use those scriptures to guide them repeatedly, until it becomes second nature. They diligently study the scriptures, become confident enough in their beliefs to apply them to real-world scenarios, and with enough repetitions, they develop an unshakable faith in them and believe without doubt that they will apply in all circumstances.

One of the most incredible displays of faith I have had to employ was when I began my MBA journey. When I finished my undergraduate degree, I knew I wanted to do something different with my life. Whether it was becoming a CEO of a multi-million dollar corporation or a successful entrepreneur making millions of dollars from the comfort of my living room, I was going to do something huge. However, I knew I needed to open up some additional doors via education and networking to do so. Therefore, I did what any recent college graduate might do: I procrastinated. Two quick years went by and I found myself stuck in that entry-level position that I did not take any pleasure in. As explained earlier, I got sick and tired of being sick and tired and resolved to do something about it. After careful planning and thought, I decided to go to school part-time.

The next three years were the longest of my life. Not only was I working long hours, but I also had to pile on studying at the graduate level. I never realized college could be this challenging! In addition, it seemed that over 90% of my fellow students were smarter than I was, and making better grades to boot. I also discovered almost every hour of my day needed to be optimized to fit everything in. My routine was to wake up, go to work, go to class, get home, work a few more hours, study, and sleep (somehow I fit in eating and showering in there). On top of that, I was volunteering in the music ministry, helping form a financial mastermind, and planning a wedding at one point. It was honestly enough to drive anyone crazy!

Many times I thought I was going to quit. At various moments I told myself I was not cut out for this program, I was doing too much at one time, and I did not have the mental capacity to handle all of these stressors. I received more D's on my tests in my MBA program than I ever had during the rest of my education combined. At one point, my grades dropped so low I was put under academic probation. All signs were pointing to me needing to either take time off to refocus or abandon the whole effort altogether.

However, I chose neither. I fully placed my faith in God, as I had in the past, in order to get me through this critical juncture. During my toughest days, I meditated on scriptures and reflected on the numerous times that I had crushed other insurmountable goals. In order to keep up my grades, I began to form weekly study groups while somehow carving out a bit more individual study time to reinforce the materials. This type of diligence was necessary to build up my confidence and keep me going. With each passing test grade, my confidence grew. With each completed course, I knew I was one step closer to my goal. In turn, I grew even more faithful that I would not be denied my degree. Finally, after three long years of struggle and effort, I graduated with a 3.56 GPA, having received all A's in three separate semesters. Had I not remained diligent in my studies and found ways of increasing my confidence, my faith would not have been sufficient and I would have likely burnt and dropped out.

When placed in proper context, it is easy to see faith as a crucial force that will deliver you into the Promised Land. On the other hand, I must warn you about placing blind faith in things, people, or even yourself. The equivalent to gambling, blind faith can cause you to travel down a dangerous rabbit hole of anguish and disappointment. Everyone makes mistakes and not everyone is looking out for your best interests. For every success story where someone has seemingly "put it all on black," there have been millions of failures. A continually successful person would not do for those odds.

Even my pastor, as well-versed as he is in scripture, instructs people not to just blindly believe him and his sermons. Instead, he cautions his congregation to go straight to the Word and read the scriptures themselves to ensure that they are in agreement with his points. Otherwise, he could really say anything while he is up in the pulpit to lead his flock to the wolves.

Faith is an amazing force because it provides support and confidence when it is needed most. Although it takes a lot of courage and initiative to act on faith, it is made easier by constant study and practice in that given area. Each time you step out of your comfort zone it will become easier, until the point where comfort does not matter as much. That is the point when you can really begin to see the results of your endeavors. It is at that point that your faith will take you to completely new levels of success.

Action Summary:
1. You must place your faith in something. Otherwise, success will elude you every time and you will not have the confidence to pursue it.
2. Faith requires confidence, and confidence requires diligence. You must dedicate yourself to your goal and devote time, energy, and practice towards developing the faith you need in that area.
3. Be wary of placing blind faith in anything unless you feel it is

necessary. A high-risk, high-reward scenario such as that more often than not will blow up in your face.

One Force Affects All Others

The amazing fact about *The 5 Essential Forces of Success* model is that it is all interconnected; meaning the improvement of one force affects them all. Each force is a cog in the machine that is success. As you turn one, another cog begins to move, causing a chain reaction down the line. Thus every cog works together to make the machine run until you reach success.

This should not come as a surprise to you. Earlier, we talked about the power of Accountability to increase both Drive and Ambition. When you hold yourself accountable to a goal, you will become motivated (one of the crucial components of Drive) to achieve it. Furthermore, holding yourself accountable to do your best will cause you to strive for more challenging goals (the essence of Ambition). You could even say that the accountable will likely create a plan to increase their chances of success and employ their faith to fight through resistance.

As another example, let us examine Drive. When you are a passionate and motivated individual, you will feel confident and ambitious enough to challenge yourself. The highly driven will also do anything to see their dreams realized, so they will take the time to prepare and study the area in which they are attempting to make gains. Their drive will also force them to be accountable to achieving their goals, and these driven individuals will likely develop the faith in themselves that it takes to achieve success.

I hope you have begun to see how powerful this model for success is. From Oprah to Madonna to Steve Jobs, all have been able to develop and utilize each one of these Essential Forces to accomplish spectacular, revolutionary, and life-changing feats. However, at some point they had to step out of their comfort zone and start developing and using these forces to possess their success. In the next chapter, I will show you how to take this leap and hit the ground running.

Take the Leap

"The danger of venturing into unchartered waters is not nearly as dangerous as staying on shore, waiting for your boat to come in." Charles F. Glassman

"I never thought I would be doing this," Cynthia began nervously, eyes anywhere but her manager's gaze. Her palms were sweating profusely, and she had to press her hands together to keep them from shaking. She had imagined this day for years, contemplating the various ways she would explain that she did not want to miss her beautiful children growing up. At the same time, fifteen years is a long time just to throw away. Yet there she was, sitting in front of her manager. She could barely bring herself to mutter the words: "Effective immediately, I quit."

Alex thought his life was over. What was he to do now? He poured his life and soul into that company, and just like that, he was laid off. All that talk about valuing employee loyalty must have meant nothing, he thought. Now how am I going to feed my kids? On his way home, Alex pondered his next steps. His resume was antiquated, and he knew that his position was in very low demand. However, he also knew that his skills were also transferrable to other areas of business. His accounting skills were at par with some CPAs, and he gained valuable experience managing and leading his team members through some very difficult transitions. Wait, he thought. Could this be the start of a new career in consulting?

The plane approached the runway, and Amit could not help but be excited. His parents always talked about India, and now he was going to see it firsthand—permanently. Many spend their lives working to leave India and settle in America, and here I am doing the opposite! Amit thought. However, Amit knew he had a special calling, and his work was to be done in his parents' native homeland. "Here is to leaving behind everything I ever knew," he whispered softly to himself as the airport quickly disappeared from sight.

What do all of these stories have in common? Each of the characters is essentially standing on a ledge. Behind them are their old, comfortable lives, full of predictability and complacency. What lies before them, however, is a glimpse into the unknown. They could have infinite amounts of success or failure, eternal happiness or endless regret. They will never know until they first take the leap.

This is what we are faced with when making life-altering decisions. I am not going to pretend that it is easy to take blind leaps of faith. However, as the Limitless, you do not search for easy opportunities; you search for opportunities that will ultimately bring you happiness and a sense of fulfillment regardless of the level of difficulty. Fear not, because in this chapter I will explain the factors to consider when taking the leap and the methods of making the landing just a little bit softer. If you are on the edge, read on.

When Should You Take the Leap?

Taking the leap, or making the decision to take on something new, intimidating, notable, challenging, and/or risky, will test you in every way possible. Taking the leap requires you to step out of your comfort zone, which is a very scary thing for many because it comes with such a deep sense of anxiety of the unknown. In many ways, it is like suffering from vertigo: your mind and senses become overwhelmed to the point that your stomach starts to turn!

This is why you should know when it makes sense to take such a seemingly large risk. Knowing when to take the leap is almost more important than knowing how to take the leap. Fortunately, there are a few telltale signs you can use to determine if you are ready for the plunge into the unknown.

When you are complacent in your current situation

"Complacency is man's biggest weakness. It creeps upon us when we least expect it." Jay Mullings

People get complacent. It happens all the time. We as humans generally enjoy stability and security, while jobs, families, and your town or city can provide these intangibles. Unfortunately, these intangibles can also become anchors that keep you from changing, innovating, or improving your situation.

It was for this very reason that I could not stay in my high school hometown of Jacksonville, Florida. Jacksonville, a beach town with a land-area that rivals some small countries, is a great place to settle down and start a family. Much of my immediate family and some of my best friends live there. However, when I evaluated the various places I would like to live, Jacksonville was near the bottom.

Although I loved Jacksonville and those who lived there, I knew deep inside that if I chose to remain there after high school, I would likely never want to leave. The security and familiarity of the city would be too alluring. Thus, after I graduated, I took the leap and left the comforts of Jacksonville to attend college. I have never regretted making the decision to leave, but it sure was not easy to do. In fact, my mother, ever reluctant to cut those apron strings, reminded me daily of the money I would be saving and the fun I would be having if I stayed at home for school. In addition to the job I ended up choosing after college, I received an offer from another firm to move back to Jacksonville and make more money. However, once I made the decision to leave, I never looked back.

Learning to leave complacency behind will make things more challenging but also constantly force you out of your comfort zone, leading to more opportunities for success. No matter what you do, if you are out of your comfort zone, you are in the right place.

When you are discontent in your current situation

"Healthy discontent is the prelude to progress." Mahatma Gandhi

Being discontent is a miserable feeling that can lead to depression, frustration, anger, and regret. If you find yourself constantly complaining about your job, your finances, or the way your life turned out, change it! Action is vital. Without it, you will never see any improvement in your situation.

Before I started this book, I was in a place of dissatisfaction in one area of my life that was extremely important to me: my ministry of music. While I still loved playing trumpet with the praise and worship team at my local church, I felt I was not growing in my musicianship or adding anything of value to the ministry. This discordant plateau began to affect both my mood and my willingness to serve. Finally, one Sunday, while playing in front of the congregation of worshippers, I realized I simply was not happy. My passion for one reason or another had been sapped from me. I was just going through the motions, and I was not helping anyone (myself included). That day, I muscled up the courage to end my misery and leave the ministry. A couple of weeks later, I found the inspiration for my book, and the rest is history.

Sometimes you need to move out of places that cause you frustration. Although it can be incredibly challenging (it took me over a year to get to the point where I was ready to take this leap), you may find that there are better things ahead of you than behind you.

When you have a fear of failure

"Success may come either by aiming at it directly or by passionately avoiding failure." Philoppos

Another sign that you are ready to take the leap is the fear of failure. Now, I know it sounds crazy, but it is the truth. When you are afraid to fail, you are more likely to take steps to ensure you do not fail. Imagine you are considering mountain climbing as a hobby. There is a realistic fear of failure there. If anything goes wrong, it could mean devastating injuries or even certain death. What do you do? Well, you could decide not to follow through on your intentions out of fear, or you could take steps to reduce the risk of failure, such as receiving proper training, purchasing proper safety equipment, and starting off with a rock gym until you develop your confidence and skills.

Remember, fear is a yield sign, not a stop sign; it is there to remind you to proceed with caution.

POSSESS YOUR SUCCESS: MASTERING THE LIMITLESS SUCESS METHOD

When you know you will procrastinate otherwise

"Procrastination makes easy things hard, hard things harder."
Mason Cooley

Procrastination is one of the biggest dream-killers I know. It is easy to fall into the snare of laziness simply because it takes minimal effort. However, taking the leap requires action. If you get into the habit of putting things off until another date, you will never get anywhere.

I was a huge procrastinator in high school. Although consistently earning good grades in my classes, I made an art out of waiting until the last minute to get anything done. The work was rarely challenging, so I knew I could afford to wait until the midnight hour to get started. When I got to college, I was shocked to learn I had lost my powers of procrastination! Every time I put off studying or working on an assignment until the last minute, I would score considerably low. I then realized that to maintain my level of success I had to either get better at working under duress or begin on my coursework earlier. Perhaps unsurprisingly, once I changed my patterns from procrastination to preparation, I was not only able to maintain my grades, but improve them dramatically.

While it may not sound like a major leap of faith, it required a considerable shift in one of the habits I had developed since grade school. I had to realize my laziness was a liability and trust that this change would make a positive impact. The key here is to get started, and get started early. Do not put off until tomorrow what you can do today.

ANDREW G. MCDONALD

When you are led to

"All our dreams can come true if we have the courage to pursue them." Walt Disney

In the Bible, God made a habit out of taking unproven, questionable, and even murderous individuals and calling them to do His will. It was always astonishing to me. I would read about these unlikely heroes and wonder to myself, "You mean there weren't any better alternatives around?" However, it is amazing what improbable individuals can do with a bit of faith and focus.

While I have stated before that it is vital to prepare for your success, it is plausible for some to put themselves in a place where failure is not an option before they begin the preparation process. When they hear their calling, they must jump into it without dwelling too much on it because they may not proceed otherwise. There is going to be more of a learning curve if you take this route, but if you apply the 5 Forces of Success along the way, you will get there much more expediently. In this case, you must sincerely judge yourself and your calling.

Do not use the fact that you "don't feel ready" as an excuse to ignore your calling. If you are being led to do something, take action! Otherwise, you may be missing the chance to live your dreams.

When Should You Not Take the Leap?

On the other hand, there are certainly times when you should not take a leap of faith. A leap of faith requires a level of discernment and maturity that many people do not have. It also requires patience, knowledge, and the thickest skin you can possibly develop. Those who possess opposing qualities, especially the qualities below, have a much higher risk of failure in their endeavors. Here is a list of signs that will tell you that you might not be as ready for that leap as you thought you were:

When you are disorganized

"Disorganization can scarcely fail to result in inefficiency." Dwight Eisenhower

Have you ever tried working at a cluttered desk? Some say that clutter does not bother them, but I do not understand how anyone can operate effectively in a messy environment. I personally become easily distracted and my work suffers greatly without organization in my area. However, once I clean up my space and begin the planning process, it is like a breath of fresh air. My focus increases dramatically and so does the quality of my output. It is as if the more order there is to my area and schedule, the more organized my mind becomes.

If you are scatter-brained or have not developed very good planning habits, you may want to consider working on this before you try to take the leap. Distractions will inevitably lure your attention away from what you were once focused on, and your disorganization will form obstacles on your way to success. De-cluttering your environment, whether physical or mental, along with forming a solid, organized plan will make you much more successful when you take that leap than those who attempt to operate in dysfunction.

ANDREW G. MCDONALD

When you are impatient

"Impatience serves as the mother of mistakes and the father of irritation." Steve Maraboli

I find that those who are most eager to get started have the highest chance of failure. They do not take the time to think about the complexity of the endeavor or the steps involved, leading to costly mistakes in judgment and execution. Worse, these same people become frustrated by the amount of attempts it takes to get things right. They think they should be able to figure it out the first time and are dismayed when success takes longer than anticipated.

Success does not come easily. It is the culmination of several attempts, years of practice, energy, focus, effort, and above all, patience. They say it takes over 10,000 hours to become a master in a given area of expertise. This means that if you were to practice something consistently for an hour a day every day, it would take over 27 years for you to achieve mastery. 27 years! Now, imagine the amount of patience required to wait 27 years for this type of success. This is why taking that leap should be more than just an impulse, and once taken, requires so much patience. True success will test your limits continually and will quickly weed out the impatient.

When you lack expertise in the given area

"An investment in knowledge pays the best interest." Benjamin Franklin

I would like to make one thing clear: you do not have to be a master to become successful in the goal you plan to achieve. In fact, many prosperous people out there began their journey before they felt they were truly ready to start. However, it does require you to be at least knowledgeable in that area.

For example, you decide you tire of your 9-to-5 gig and wish to become an entrepreneur. You have always wanted to open and manage your own restaurant, but to date have had zero experience in the food service industry and you have somehow made it possible to burn water. Would it be a great idea to quit your job and lease or purchase space for your new career as a restaurant owner? No! The learning curve would be too high, since you have no knowledge about the domain you want to enter into. Instead, you would want to take culinary classes and gain some experience inside a restaurant before you make such a bold move. This would bring clarity to deciding if this is the way you really want to go.

Now, this is not to discourage you from achieving your dreams because you feel you do not know enough. On the other hand, you have to know enough to get started and/or have the willingness to learn. Otherwise, your dreams will be dead in the water.

<u>When you do not have a plan of attack</u>

"Planning is bringing the future into the present so you can do something about it." Alan Lakein

In the previous chapter, I discussed at length the importance of having a plan for your success. Continual success requires proper planning; there is no way around it. How are you going to take that leap? What is needed to do so? Is there a contingency plan for when you encounter turbulence, obstacles, or resistance? These are all factors you will need to consider when creating a plan of attack for your leap.

ANDREW G. MCDONALD

Taking the leap without a plan is akin to jumping out of a plane without a parachute. It is a terrible idea, which is likely not to end well for you.

When your heart is not in it

"It is your passion that empowers you to be able to do that thing you were created to do." TD Jakes

Sometimes you do not want to take that leap, not because you are afraid or feel you are not ready, but because you are just not passionate enough to achieve success in that area. This is OK. You should not have to pursue something you are not passionate about, and doing so will lead to an abundance of mistakes, regret, frustration, and unhappiness. Joy comes in feeling fulfilled, and if you spend the many precious hours of your day working towards something that is not fulfilling, then it is a complete waste of effort.

When I was in high school, the U.S. Marines heavily recruited me. I never saw myself as a military type of person, but the benefits were definitely attractive to me. At the time, I was also exploring music as a possible career, and they explained I could actually audition as a Marine bandsman. My school would be paid for, I could enter as an officer, and I would be doing something I loved to do. My military test scores were very high as well, and it seemed like I was all but set to become a Marine.

Why, then, did I have such reluctance to committing to one of the most prestigious branches of the U.S. military? It was as if a voice in the back of my head was repeating, "Andrew, you know that this is not for you. This is not what you want to be doing for the rest of your life." This voice grew to such a level that I could no longer ignore it. When I sat down in front of my parents and the recruiter for what was supposed to be a discussion about my military intentions, I looked into each one of their eyes and confessed, "I am sorry, but I just cannot do this." My recruiter looked as if I had just slapped him in the face, and after few curt parting words to my parents and me, he stormed out of our home and drove off.

You see, even though I would have likely made a fine Marine, I knew it then and I know it now that I would never have fully enjoyed the experience. Life is too short to waste time on the things that do not bring you joy, and you should never take the leap without assurance of that critical emotional component.

Be a Feather, Not a Rock

"It was not raining when Noah built the ark." Howard Ruff

Now that we have evaluated when you should and should not take the leap, it is time to ensure that when you do, you hit the ground running.

If you were in a free fall, would you rather be a feather or a rock? A feather, light as can be, will float effortlessly and land softly to the ground unharmed. A much heavier rock, on the other hand, will plummet straight down to the ground, and depending on its weight and the height it falls from, could smash into pieces upon impact.

The best method of becoming that feather is to plan your leap effectively. This may seem obvious, but many people wait until they feel they cannot stand their current situation any longer to finally take action, and their decisions at that point are usually rash. This sort of knee-jerk reaction typically leads to undue pain and setbacks later on, such as extra stress and self-doubt. If you have a dead-end job you do not like, you do not want to wait until you cannot stand another minute there to determine your next move. At that point, you might be liable to blow up on someone or quit on the spot, burning bridges in the process. Instead, you want to plot your escape long before you get to that critical juncture. A wise individual once said it best: "Do what is difficult when times are easy. Otherwise, you will suffer when times are difficult."

To that point, you are also going to want to think about how you will fund your initiative before you begin. Money is a very important matter, and a good grasp of financial management will go a long way towards keeping you afloat. This does not just apply to aspiring entrepreneurs, either. A big career change might require additional formal education and training, increasing your costs. Raising a child is one of the most expensive endeavors you could undertake. Whatever the leap is for you, chances are that you are going to need to have some cash handy to support it along with supporting yourself.

It is advisable that you have some sort of nest egg in place to fall back on, usually between 3-6 months' worth of expenses. If something goes wrong or you are terminated from your job (either voluntary or otherwise), that nest egg will be a lifesaver. Simply set aside some money from every paycheck to your dream fund and teach yourself not to touch it. It may be difficult at first, but if you practice diligence and restraint, it is very doable. Remember, if you consistently focus your thoughts and words on your goals, temptation will not triumph.

POSSESS YOUR SUCCESS: MASTERING THE LIMITLESS SUCESS METHOD

Another effective step to ensure your leap is graceful is to gather support for your cause. Remember, you are just one person. You may not be able to tackle every obstacle you encounter on your own, and maybe you should not. It takes a village to raise a child, and addictions are rarely defeated by those who rely solely on their own strength and self-effort to make the permanent change they need. However, the support of your friends, family, and others loyal to you will make a consistent, lasting impact on you which you can use to influence others.

What many other successful people use is a three-fold system of support to make their leaps that much easier. The first layer of support comes from those above you: your mentors, your heroes, and your models of success. These individuals have already been through the anxiety, the struggles, the pitfalls, and the pain you may have to contend with after your leap. You may never meet some of these individuals, but they are still able to use their stories and experiences to help lift you up to your next level. You also should look to them as an inspiration, a real-life image of what is in store for you. Utilizing this top layer in this way will fully accelerate your growth.

The second layer of your support is made up of your peers. These are your contacts, friends, and acquaintances that are on your same level of success and will keep you accountable to your goals. Since they are on your level, you can relate to each other's successes and struggles, thereby fostering a sense of comradery. They can also provide tips and tricks that they are learning as well as provide a fresh perspective on your situation that you or the top layer may not have thought of previously.

Finally, your third layer of support is comprised of your admirers and mentees, those up–and-comers who want to learn from you and your experiences. This third layer is necessary to solidify your understanding or skills, as well as to help keep you on your toes. Becoming an expert in a certain area can sometimes lead to becoming complacent over time and losing the drive that got you to that status. Having less-seasoned followers watching and studying your every move will help motivate you to continue improving and growing.

If you are just starting out in your quest for Limitless success, then it is perfectly fine to only acquire the top two layers of support and develop your third layer as you go. Trust me, if your success is important enough, others will become naturally curious of your methods. The key here is to ensure that you build up this third layer of support in some way, either directly or indirectly. This layer will certainly want to see you succeed because you are currently where they want to be; in essence, your success will be their success.

Unfortunately, not everyone will jump on your Limitless bandwagon. If you are taking the leap into something controversial or uncommon, you will encounter some form of resistance. People will caution you to follow the crowd and adhere to conventional wisdom. They may not see the potential in you or share your vision, and instead want to push you towards their agenda. Others may wish to protect you from harm or failure, touting their experience or credibility as justification for shooting you down. Still others may belittle you, as if your goal or dream is nothing but a foolish wish that will never materialize.

This is all natural. Simply keep in mind that in order for the Limitless Success Method to work, you must be willing to do the things others do not normally do. Dave Ramsey, the financial freedom guru, in fact stated, "If you live like no one else, later you will live like no one else." It is normal to carry debt. It is normal to eat unhealthy foods. It is normal to hate your job and live life unfulfilled. Does this mean we should accept this as the status quo?

The dream-killers and the haters act like anchors that continually pull you down, making it difficult to gain any traction and increasing your chances of failure. In many cases, the only way to remedy this situation is to let the dead weights go. It is time to reduce your contact with these people. You must protect your dreams and goals at all costs, and these two groups of people will likely become threats with which to contend. I like to think of it this way: if you cannot change your circle, then it is time to change your circle. Simply put, if you find you cannot influence the negative individuals around you, you should look for other positive ones to be around.

Earlier I described the Structural Tension Theory and how we can wind up in oscillating patterns. Relationships can have this very same effect on us. We want to take a leap of faith on our dreams, so we begin to move forward. Negative influences resist and convince us otherwise, so we begin to move backward. This happens repeatedly over time until we wear out and give up. If we can simply reduce the amount of interference running, we will triumph over the naysayers.

Moreover, you can use doubters to propel you forward, similarly to how a slingshot works. Their negative thoughts and words act as the tension for the slingshot, but if you can ignore them and hold them off long enough, they will eventually have no choice but to relent, shooting you forward with such speed that they have no hope of stopping you. It is a way to repurpose negative energy for your benefit, and it is extremely effective. It also has the added bonus of using your haters' tricks and tactics against them, burning them in the process. According to the great Mahatma Gandhi, "first they ignore you, then they laugh at you, then they fight you, then you win."

As you continue in your journey to become Limitless and rack up successes, you will become much more confident, and taking the leap will begin to become easier. Of course, in the beginning things will be new and frightening. However, this does not mean that we should never press forward and experience all that God has to offer. From this point on, your life may never get easier, but with experience and following these tips, you will be winning without limits in no time.

Conclusion: How to Enjoy Your Success

Let us envision for a moment that you have employed the Limitless Success Method precisely and have finally possessed success in your goals and dreams. You have poured your blood, sweat, and tears into your endeavors and taken advantage of every opportunity to advance your agenda. You harnessed the power of thoughts, visualization, words, and actions and it is demonstrated in the results. The culmination of all the hard work and strategic planning is finally here, and only one question remains: "Now what?"

This is the question that plagued me every time I achieved a goal or a given task. As soon as I crossed the finish line, a huge wave of exuberance washed over me, followed by an equally huge wave of dread. I felt lost and helpless with no sense of direction, and the only thing that would cheer me up would be to set an even bigger challenge.

I soon realized that this was an unsustainable path. At some point the highs wouldn't be as high, and the lows would become too low to endure. Another, more astonishing revelation hit me soon after: I was not giving myself the chance to enjoy my success. As hard as I had worked to accomplish a given goal, I never took the time to reflect on what I accomplished.

The Limitless may have a tough time overcoming this problem. It is easy for those who are goal-focused and driven to move on without giving themselves a chance to rest, relax, and reflect. Ignoring this will ultimately lead to burnout, increased and unnecessary failures, and even depression. These are not experiences you should be having after achieving your victories!

Take Beyoncé, currently one of the most prominent music artists to grace the stage with her presence. She has put thousands of hours of effort into developing her impressive vocal abilities, her electric choreographed dance routines, and her overall "femme-power" brand. Though she has traveled the world many times during her illustrious career, most of her experiences only involved the inside of her transportation, her hotel room, and her venue. Many within the industry know her as a workaholic who can't seem to stay away from a recording booth even while on vacation, and up until 2010 that perception held true. "I had talked about taking a vacation before," Beyoncé intimated in her interview with Essence magazine back in 2012, "but always ended up in the studio after two weeks, so no one believed me."

Finally determined to take the break she so desperately needed, she swore herself away from any productions for nearly a whole year to focus on her emotional and mental state while avoiding burnout. During her hiatus, she traveled, went to concerts, and learned how to cook a decent meal. Beyoncé viewed it as both a break to recover from the rigors of her everyday life as well as an opportunity to find inspiration for later projects.

Now, we can't all be like Beyoncé and travel the world first class, but there are definitely tangible actions we can all take to balance our drive for goal achievement with our satisfaction from the results. Therefore, I derived this list of five steps you can take to enjoy the success you have been blessed with and toiled so diligently for. Plainly said, if you cannot take delight in your success, then what is the point?

Pay it Forward First

This principle was discussed at length during the second chapter of this book but applies in a big way here. I discussed the unpleasant concept of financial constipation, as well as how PFF from the very beginning will make your success that much more fulfilling. Again, you may not have the financial means to give, which is fine; simply find other means of paying it forward, either through the donations of your time or effort. Often, you will have a much bigger impact on others with an hour of your time than you will with a large amount of money.

Humility and Thankfulness

What do you visualize in your mind when you think of uber-successful celebrities? Is it the red carpet, designer clothes and accessories, or millions of dollars in cars and assets? Most people also think of egotism and snobbery reserved only for the highest of aristocrats. However, what people least envision is the small group of celebrities who live their lives filled with utmost graciousness and meekness.

No matter how successful we become or how much influence we might gain over time, without balancing them with gratitude and humility we will be at risk of living a miserable life. Humility reminds us of where we came from, while thankfulness teaches us to appreciate how far we have come. It is easy for people to forget how to tap into these two emotions on their rise to the top of whatever summit they are aspiring to, which is why you must practice humility early on.

ANDREW G. MCDONALD

One of the most influential and yet humble individuals that comes to mind is Bono, the lead singer of U2. The band, since its inception in the late 1970's, has earned countless accolades, including Grammys, American Music Awards, and various international awards as well. As powerful and popular as he has become, Bono has somehow never lost his sense of poise and grace. He minimalizes his ego by being very socially conscious, leading fights against world poverty, AIDS, and hunger, among many other causes.

In fact, Tony Campolo, an author and international speaker, recounted a perfect illustration of Bono's humbleness. He was asked to speak at an English Christian music arts festival, of which Bono was an attendee. Many times, people informed Bono of his striking resemblance to the U2 bandsman, to which he replied: "I hear that often. That's why I bought these shades, to complete the look." Furthermore, when the event's organizers needed help with handling their parking situation, Bono sprang into action, not by delegating or supervising, but by jumping in on the frontlines, directing traffic! His willingness to serve is a shining demonstration of his grounded personality and his graciousness.

Be Content, Not Complacent

Possessing humility and thankfulness are two ways you can be content with your life and your current situation. Both the Limited and Limitless struggle with this concept of contentment because they are either too focused on the negatives of their present circumstances or too concerned about contentment as a means to complacency. However, understanding the difference between contentment and complacency is in reality a major factor in enjoying your success.

POSSESS YOUR SUCCESS: MASTERING THE LIMITLESS SUCESS METHOD

When you are content, it is true that you are happy with your progress and you can see just how far you have come. This is positive, because through contentment you learn to appreciate the struggles and trials you have had to overcome thus far to get to where you are today. From there, we can experience joy and peacefulness on completely different levels than we could previously.

On the other hand, what we must be cognizant of is becoming stagnant in our growth and development. One of the best examples of complacency in business today is the camera film business. For decades, camera film companies were at the top of their game. The future was bright and they were content with their profits. They never saw new technologies like camera phones and digital imaging coming, and before they knew it, their entire competitive landscape shifted. Although many are still around, these companies had to completely change how they did business to survive, as camera film is nowhere near as profitable as it used to be.

Fortunately, with gratitude and humility, you can enjoy your victories while keeping stock of your drive to keep moving forward. We all need a break at times, and a plateau in performance is normal. On the other hand, it is when one becomes comfortable and settles for less than their best when caution should be exercised. It is a very challenging balance that can only be achieved with constant reflection and wisdom on what your goals are and how you aspire to achieve them.

ANDREW G. MCDONALD

Celebrate Your Victories

It is such a rush to complete something you previously thought you could never do. Your adrenaline kicks in, your emotions surge to an all-time high, and you may even shed a tear or two, depending on how personal the goal was to you. However, for people like me, the high only lasts for a fleeting moment before I proceed to achieve another one of my "impossible" goals, leading to a lower drive and ultimately burnout. This is why celebrating your victories is so important: it forces you to take some time to acknowledge your hard work before you get back to the grind again.

For instance, many people set weight goals to improve their physique and their health that involve rigorous training and a rigid, unappealing diet of low-carb, high-protein foods. However, the true success stories always incorporate a "cheat day" once every so often, as well as rewards for achieving milestones towards that overall goal. These incentives are very controlled so as not to backslide into their previous habits but provide a valuable and necessary outlet to relieve stress and prevent an all-out abandonment of the quest to lose weight.

These cheat days and rewards will work in almost every aspect of goal-setting and achievement as well. For example, in the writing of this book, I set a goal of writing 500 words per day, four times per week, until it was complete. Once every six to eight weeks, I gave myself the week off to relax my mind and enjoy what I had accomplished thus far. In addition, once the book is in print, I plan on taking one month's time off before pursuing any other endeavors to recuperate and celebrate the victory of writing my first book. In each of these examples, the reward is controlled and defined in advance to avoid a disruption in drive.

Have Fun along the Way

The last piece of advice I have to conclude this book is to have fun! It may seem trivial, but why should you have to work so hard if you cannot have fun while you are doing it? This does not mean every aspect of your journey will be fun. In fact, it will likely be filled with difficulty and strife. However, you can take pleasure in the midst of pain because you are learning, growing, and progressing. Holding your head up high and smiling even when it hurts are two excellent ways of convincing your mind that success is around the corner and you are "having fun" even if it doesn't quite feel like it.

It also helps to journal your successes and struggles while you are in the middle of them. Back in 2010, I came up with the idea of creating a blog, PossessYourSuccess.com, for the purposes of journaling my path to success. In it I desired to chronicle my thoughts and experiences as I set goals, encountered obstacles, and overcame them. Going back through some of my earlier writings actually helps me enjoy my current circumstances because I remind myself of all the benefits I have previously received by working through those tribulations.

Do not wait until the end to enjoy your hard work. Enjoy it now, and your path will seem that much easier for you.

In truth, possessing your success is tough. It takes work, grit, and the right opportunities to make it happen. Defining what success is for you, making the commitment to realizing that vision, and enjoying that success when it materializes are even more challenging. However, the Limitless Success Method works, and it works well. Apply it to one small goal in your life simply as a test. Furthermore, remember that your overall success or contribution to this world does not have to be some major pinnacle of an accomplishment

ANDREW G. MCDONALD

that will change millions of lives. Focus on changing one life (even if that one life is yours) and that will suffice. In that spirit, I leave you with this parable of the boy and the starfish:

> A man was walking along a deserted beach at sunset. As he walked he could see a young boy in the distance, and as he drew nearer he noticed that the boy kept bending down, picking something up and throwing it into the water.
>
> Time and again he kept hurling things into the ocean.
>
> As the man approached even closer, he was able to see that the boy was picking up starfish that had been washed up on the beach and, one at a time, he was throwing them back into the water.
>
> The man asked the boy what he was doing, and the boy replied, "I am throwing these washed up starfish back into the ocean, or else they will die through lack of oxygen."
>
> "You can't possibly save them all. There are thousands on this beach, and this must be happening on hundreds of beaches along the coast," said the man. "You can't possibly make a difference."
>
> The boy looked down, frowning for a moment, then bent down to pick up another starfish, smiling as he threw it back into the sea. He replied,
>
> "I made a huge difference to that one!"

ACETO, CHRIS. "Lose More Weight with Cheat Days." http://www.muscleandfitness.com/nutrition/lose-fat/do-what-pros-do-eat-more-lose-more.

Alpert, Joel. "Interview with Joel Alpert." By Andrew McDonald (2015).

Barrysanders.com. "Barry Sanders Bio | Detroit Lions." http://www.barrysanders.com/pages/bio.

Berman, Zach. "Eagles' Sproles Achieves Big with a Small Frame." Published electronically November 22, 2014. http://articles.philly.com/2014-09-22/sports/54165476_1_darren-sproles-football-player-nfl-network.

Britannica, The Editors of Encyclopædia. "Barry Sanders." http://www.britannica.com/biography/Barry-Sanders.

Carey, Benedict. "The Mind of a Hypochondriac." Health (Time Inc. Health) 10, no. 6 (1996): 82.

"Columbine High School Shooting." 1p. 1: World Book, Inc., 2014.

Dictionary.com. "Ambition." Dictionary.com, http://dictionary.reference.com/browse/ambition?s=t.

———. "Drive." Dictionary.com, http://dictionary.reference.com/browse/drive?s=t.

———. "Faith." Dictionary.com, http://dictionary.reference.com/browse/faith?s=t.

———. "Preparation." Dictionary.com, http://dictionary.reference.com/browse/preparation?s=t.

———. "Success." Dictionary.com, http://dictionary.reference.

com/browse/success?s=t.

Eagles, Philadelphia. "Rb | Darren Sproles." Philadelphia Eagles, http://media.philadelphiaeagles.com/media/153098/sproles-darren.pdf.

Editors, Biography.com. "Barry Sanders Biography." A&E Television Networks, http://www.biography.com/people/barry-sanders-39283.

Elizabeth F. Loftus, John C. Palmer. "Reconstruction of Automobile Destruction: An Example of the Interaction between Language and Memory." Journal of Verbal Learning and Verbal Behavior 13 (1974): 585-89.

"Ellen Degeneres." The Biography.com website., http://www.biography.com/people/ellen-degeneres-9542420.

ESPN. "Darren Sproles." ESPN Internet Ventures, http://espn.go.com/nfl/player/_/id/8544/darren-sproles.

Garber, Greg. "Greg Garber Examines 5-Foot-6 Darren Sproles and Other Small Nfl Players." Published electronically November 1, 2009. http://sports.espn.go.com/nfl/playoffs2008/columns/story?columnist=garber_greg&id=3819466.

Gollwitzer, Peter M., Paschal Sheeran, Verena Michalski, and Andrea E. Seifert. "When Intentions Go Public: Does Social Reality Widen the Intention-Behavior Gap?". Psychological Science (Wiley-Blackwell) 20, no. 5 (2009): 612-18.

GoStanford.com. "Barry Sanders." http://www.gostanford.com/ViewArticle.dbml?ATCLID=208167717.

Jetten, Jolanda, and Matthew J. Hornsey. "The Line between Conformity and Resistance." Psychologist 28, no. 1 (2015): 72-74.

jrank.org. "Barry Sanders Biography - Slow Starter, Triumphed in the Nfl." http://biography.jrank.org/pages/2822/Sanders-Barry.html.

Knowles, Beyoncé. "Beyoncé Knowles' Nyabj Award-Winning Essence Article: 'Eat, Play, Love'." Published electronically May 3, 2012. http://www.essence.com/2012/05/03/beyonce-knowles-nyabj-award-essence-article-eat-play-love.

Loftus, Elizabeth F. "When a Lie Becomes Memory's Truth: Memory Distortion after Exposure to Misinformation." Current Directions in Psychological Science (Wiley-Blackwell) 1, no. 4 (1992): 121-23.

"Martin Luther King - I Have a Dream Speech - August 28, 1963." 17:28, 2011.

NFL.com. "Barry Sanders." (2015). http://www.nfl.com/player/barrysanders/2502817/profile.

———. "Darren Sproles." http://www.nfl.com/player/darrensproles/2506467/profile.

Online, Encyclopedia Britannica. "Barry Sanders | Biography."

Pro-Football-Reference.com. "Barry Sanders Nfl Football Statistics." http://www.pro-football-reference.com/players/S/SandBa00.htm.

Rotoworld. "Darren Sproles | Running Back." http://www.rotoworld.com/player/nfl/3221/darren-sproles.

"Running Back Barry Sanders." Pro Football Hall of Fame, http://www.profootballhof.com/hof/member.aspx?PLAYER_ID=187.

Russell, Cyndi. "The Boy and the Starfish." http://dreampo-

www.ingramcontent.com/pod-product-compliance
Lightning Source LLC
Chambersburg PA
CBHW070246190526
45169CB00001B/320